X-mas present to Master Nirmal

from
Manickavasagar.

GCSE Statistics

The Revision Guide

Whatever subject you're doing it's the same old story — there are lots of facts and you've just got to learn them. GCSE Statistics is no different.

Happily this CGP book gives you all that important information as clearly and concisely as possible.

It's also got some daft bits in to try and make the whole experience at least vaguely entertaining for you.

Contents

Section One — Data Collection

Section Two — Tabulation & Representation

Section Three — Data Analysis

Section Four — Probability

Published by Coordination Group Publications Ltd.

Contributors: Andrew Ballard, Sally Gill, Sharon Keeley, Val Malcolm, Sam Norman, Andy Park, Katherine Reed, Alan Rix, Mark Turner, Julie Wakeling, Sharon Watson, Janet West

ISBN-10: 1 84146 413 9
ISBN-13: 978 1 84146 413 8

Groovy website: www.cgpbooks.co.uk

With thanks to Vicky Daniel and Glenn Rogers for the proofreading.

Printed by Elanders Hindson, Newcastle upon Tyne.

Data Sources

There are two types of data source you need to know about.

Primary Data is Raw Data

Primary data is any data that hasn't been interpreted by anyone yet (i.e. raw data).

That could be:
1) data you collect especially for your project, e.g. from SURVEYS, QUESTIONNAIRES, EXPERIMENTS, etc.
2) data from a database that hasn't been processed in any way, e.g. CENSUS DATA.

Examples:
a) Jane needs to investigate the shopping habits in her local town. She collects data by using a questionnaire in the high street.
b) Peter uses the 2001 census to find out about types of employment in his area.

Secondary Data Comes from Other Sources

Secondary data will definitely have been collected by someone else.

1) It's any processed information that you find in BOOKS, DATABASES, INTERNET PAGES, MAGAZINES, NEWSPAPERS, etc.
2) It often comes in tables or graphs.
3) It could have been collected for a completely DIFFERENT REASON from yours.

Examples:
a) When Jane investigates the shopping habits in her local town she could use charts from the evening paper.
b) Peter could use a report written by the careers service to find out about employment in his local area.

Your bar chart, madam

Secondary data must be Handled with Care

Secondary data is often biased, so BE CAREFUL.

For example: It's no good using the Frogatt's Fine Foods customer shopping habits survey to find out the shopping habits of everyone in your town — not everyone shops at Frogatt's Fine Foods.

Always ask yourself these questions when dealing with secondary data:
1) Is the data RELEVANT to what you want to find out?
2) Is your source of secondary data RELIABLE and ACCURATE — is the data BIASED?

The Acid Test:

Learn the difference between primary and secondary data sources and the reasons for handling secondary data with care.

Then answer these questions.

1) You want to find out the average age of the cars in your town. Give an example of: a) a primary data source, and b) a secondary data source.
2) Tim uses data from three local car dealerships to find out the average age of the cars in his town. Give two criticisms of this method.

Types of Data

You need to know the differences between types of data.

Data can be Qualitative or Quantitative

Quantitative Data Measures Quantities

1) Quantitative data is anything that you can measure with a number.
2) For example heights of people, the time taken to complete a task, weights of things, etc.
3) Quantitative data tends to be easier to analyse than qualitative data.

Qualitative Data is Descriptive

1) Qualitative data doesn't use numbers — it's completely descriptive.
2) For example eye colour, hair colour, etc.
3) Qualitative data is quite often subjective (depending on people's opinions) — e.g. are someone's eyes hazel or brown?
   So this sort of data is usually less reliable than quantitative data.

Discrete or Continuous — Can you Measure it Exactly?

QUANTITATIVE DATA can be broken up into discrete and continuous data.
You need to understand which is which.

1) **DISCRETE DATA CAN BE MEASURED EXACTLY.**

   Your data's discrete if it represents something that's countable.
   Examples are the number of points scored in a game or the number of people going into a particular shop between 9 a.m. and midday on a Saturday morning.

2) **CONTINUOUS DATA CAN ONLY BE MEASURED TO A GIVEN DEGREE OF ACCURACY.**

   Your data's continuous if you can't measure the exact value.

   For example — the height of a block
   Say you measured the height of a block as 56 cm to the nearest centimetre. That isn't an EXACT value — you'd get a more accurate height if you measured to the nearest mm or 0.1 mm or 0.01 mm, etc. But you'll never get an exact value for its height, because there'll always be a more accurate way of measuring than the one you use.

   Other examples are the weight of an object and the time taken to do something.

The Acid Test:

Learn the definitions of quantitative, qualitative, discrete and continuous data. Turn over the page and write them down.

1) Say whether this data is qualitative, discrete quantitative or continuous quantitative:
   a) The number of spectators at a rugby match.
   b) The time taken to get to school by each student in Year 9.
   c) The colours of pebbles on a beach.
   d) The lengths of fish in Windermere.
   e) The nationalities of people visiting a museum on a certain day.
   f) The number of times each student in class 11A is late for school in a given month.

Classifying Data

Once you've collected data you need to start processing it.

You can Split your Data into Classes

A good first step when you've got loads of raw data is to split it into different CLASSES. When you do this, it's important that you DEFINE THE CLASSES WELL — so you know exactly which class to put each bit of data in.
Here's how NOT to do it:

> A student divides the colour of mice into the following classes:
>
> White, Grey, Greyish white, Brown, Black/Brown and Black
>
> The classes are badly defined because they overlap. The decision of which class to put each mouse into depends on who makes it — it's subjective.

You can skip the rest of this page if you're doing AQA

You can put your Data onto Different Types of Scale

1) **Categorical scales** — if you've got qualitative data, it's sometimes useful to give your classes a number to make it easier to process the data.
   For example, you might split eye colour into 'blue', 'brown' and 'other'.
   You could number the 'blue' class 1, the 'brown' class 2 and the 'other' class 3.
   The numbers can't be used for anything other than labelling the classes — they don't have any other meaning.
2) **Rank scales** — here numbers are given to classes, but they are only used to order a list.
   For example, a survey could ask people to rank celebrities' attractiveness from 0 (very unattractive) to 5 (very attractive). The difference between a 2 and a 3 might not be the same as the difference between a 4 and a 5.

Higher

3) **Interval scales** — here, equal steps on the scale do mean something.
   An important example is temperature, where the difference between 10 °C and 20 °C is the same as the difference between 30 °C and 40 °C. But an interval scale doesn't have a true zero, so you can't say that 20 °C is twice as hot as 10 °C.
4) **Ratio scales** — these are "proper scales". Equal steps on the scale mean something and the measurements have a true zero.
   For example two kilometres is twice as far as one kilometre.
   Other examples of ratio scales are areas, volumes and data that can be counted.

The Acid Test:

Learn the different ways to divide up your data, then cover the page up and write it all down.

1) Which type of scale would be best for the following sets of data — categorical, rank, interval or ratio?
   a) The distance walked by each student to the school canteen.
   b) Marks out of 10 given by each student for the tastiness of their school lunch.
   c) The temperatures of the school lunches eaten by students.
   d) Type of school lunch bought by each student (sandwich, chips, beefburger, etc.)

More Types of Data

Grouping data — when the Spread of Data's too Big

If you measured the ages of 50 people living on a street, you'd probably get data that's really spread out (e.g. anything from 0-110). You might need to group the data to make it more manageable:

Age in completed years	0 - 19	20 - 39	40 - 59	60 - 79	80 and over
Number of people	6	13	14	8	9

1) The groups in a frequency table are called CLASS INTERVALS, or CLASS WIDTHS. So in the table above, the class intervals are 0-19, 20-39, etc.
2) The LOWER CLASS LIMITS (or CLASS BOUNDARIES) are 0, 20, 40, ...
3) The UPPER CLASS LIMITS are 19, 39, 59, ... (See p.25)

The problem with grouping data is that you don't know what the exact data values are any more, which means you have to ESTIMATE statistics like the MEAN and MEDIAN (see Section 3).

Bivariate data — measuring 2 things

EXAMPLE: This table shows the heights and weights of 10 students.

Student	A	B	C	D	E	F	G	H	I	J
Height (m)	1.34	2.01	1.70	1.51	1.49	1.76	1.85	1.69	1.68	1.49
Weight (kg)	56	77	60	56	54	68	67	65	66	58

In this set of data, each student has had two data items (or variables) measured — height and weight. This type of data is called BIVARIATE — bi for two, variate for variables.

Bivariate data can be: 1) DISCRETE, 2) CONTINUOUS, 3) GROUPED, 4) UNGROUPED.

Examples: 1) Discrete bivariate data — marks out of 20 in a French test and a Maths test for a class of 30 students.

2) Continuous bivariate data — the weight and tail length of 25 cats.

When you're collecting a lot of bivariate data, you could group it. The table below shows grouped data on the weights of students and the number of hours they spend watching TV every week.

Weight (nearest kg) of students	Number of hours spent watching TV each week (nearest hour)				
	14 or fewer	15 - 19	20 - 24	25 or more	Total
Less than 50	1	0	0	0	1
50 - 59	8	7	1	1	17
60 - 69	3	12	4	0	19
70 - 79	1	4	7	4	16
80 or more	0	0	2	5	7
Total	13	23	14	10	60

You need to be able to interpret tables like this. For example there are 12 students who weigh 60 – 69 kg and who watch 15 – 19 hours of TV every week. The total number of students who watch 20 – 24 hours of TV every week is 14.

The Acid Test:

Learn what these things mean: class limits, class intervals, bivariate data.

1) Look at the weight/TV table above.
   a) What is the total number of students who weigh 70 – 79 kg?
   b) How many students who weigh 80 kg or more watch 20 – 24 hours of TV each week?

Census Data

Population — the Group you Want to Find Out About

For any statistical project, you need to find out information about a group of people or things. This group is called the population.

Examples of populations are:

1) All the pupils in a school
2) All people who have access to the internet
3) All the boxes of cereal produced by a factory
4) All the newts living in a pond.

A Census surveys Every Member of the Population

When you collect data about every member of a population, it's called a CENSUS.
This *can* be easy, but it usually isn't.
Here are some examples of populations where it's easy to carry out a census:

1) *Finding out how long it takes every student in a class to get to school in the morning. The population is all the students in the class, so you just ask them.*
2) *Finding out the Maths exam results for all the students in one year group of a school. The population is all the students in the year group — the school keeps a record of all exam results, so that's easy as well.*

These are examples of SMALL, WELL-DEFINED POPULATIONS (meaning it's easy to tell exactly who or what is in them).

A Census isn't always Practical or even Possible

Doing a census can be quite hard. (In case you didn't spot it — that was understatement.)

1) *Suppose you're trying to collect data on the lengths of newts living in a large pond. How will you know that you've surveyed all the newts in the pond?*
2) *The population census in Britain is only taken every ten years. That's because the population's SO LARGE it takes that long to count everyone and make sense of all the data. The really difficult bit is making sure everyone's been counted once and ONLY once (and they probably don't manage it).*
3) *If a battery manufacturer wanted to find out how long their batteries lasted, it wouldn't be sensible to carry out a census. The population's FAR TOO BIG (and they wouldn't have any batteries left to sell!)*

So for LARGE POPULATIONS, CENSUSES AREN'T USUALLY PRACTICAL.

The Acid Test:

Learn what's on this page, then answer this question.

1) What would the population be for the following statistical projects? Would it be sensible to carry out a census?
   a) Finding out the income of people who live on a certain street.
   b) Finding out how much time 16-year-olds in the UK spend watching TV every day.

Sampling

It isn't always practical or even possible to collect information using a census.
Instead you have to use sampling.

Sampling — a Cheap and Easy Alternative to a Census

When it isn't practical to survey a whole population, you could survey a SAMPLE instead.
Examples:

1) A battery manufacturer is challenged to check its claims that its batteries last longer than any other brand. They can't test every single battery, so they test a SAMPLE of 1000 batteries instead.
2) To find out about the amount of time spent watching TV by the people who live in a large city, a market research company surveys a SAMPLE of 2500 people.
3) Pete needs to find out about the heights of trees in a forest for his biology project. He surveys a SAMPLE of 500 trees.

Sample Data and Census Data are Different

Some ADVANTAGES of using sample data over census data are:

1) It's often more PRACTICAL to collect.
2) It's CHEAPER.
3) It's QUICKER.

The DISADVANTAGE of using sample data is that you don't have information about EVERY MEMBER of a population. It's really important to make sure the sample is REPRESENTATIVE of the population.
There are different ways of doing this — I'll tell you about those on the next few pages — but for now, here are some samples that AREN'T representative of their population:

1) In a survey to find out the average age of cars in a town, a sample was taken of 1000 cars crossing a certain roundabout between 8 a.m. and 9 a.m. on a Monday morning. This sample is likely to be mostly people on their way to work, whose cars might be newer than those of, say, pensioners.
2) A survey on the incomes of people in a town uses a sample of 10 households in a certain street. There are two things wrong with this sample:
   - it's likely that the people on the street will have similar incomes
   - it's far too small. When choosing samples, size matters — basically, the bigger your sample, the better. Any statistics (e.g. mean, variance, etc.) that you work out from a bigger sample are likely to be closer to those of the whole population.

Obviously even if two samples are representative of a population, the data (and hence any statistics you calculate) won't be exactly the same. This is called the variability between samples.

The Acid Test:

Learn everything on this page, then answer the question below.

1) Are these samples likely to be representative?
   a) A survey on the music listening preferences of a school uses a Year 7 class as a sample.
   b) A health survey of people in a hospital area uses 2500 randomly selected households in the area.

Sampling

First Make Sure your Population is Well Defined

Before you do anything else on a statistical project, you need to be clear about WHAT YOU'RE TRYING TO FIND OUT.
Once you know this, your next step is to decide exactly what your population is.
You need to put together a SAMPLE FRAME — that's a list or map of all the members of the population.

Here are some examples of well-defined populations and their sample frames:

EXAMPLE 1:
You're trying to find out the average Key Stage 3 SATs score for Maths in England in 2003. Your population would be all students in England who took the Key Stage 3 Maths SAT in 2003. Your sample frame would be a list of all students who took the Key Stage 3 Maths SAT in 2003.

EXAMPLE 2:
Ahliah needs to find out the average height of the chestnut trees in her local country park for a science project. The population she uses is all the chestnut trees in the country park. Instead of listing the trees, Ahliah makes a map of the country park with all the chestnut trees marked and uses that as her sample frame.

Simple Random Sampling — Sampling without Bias

Once you've decided on your population and made a sample frame, you need to choose a sample that represents the population FAIRLY (without BIAS).

With relatively small, well-defined populations, you can use a SIMPLE RANDOM SAMPLE. In a simple random sample, every member of the population has an EQUAL chance of being chosen.

EXAMPLE: If your population was the 2000 students who go to Eastfield Secondary School, your sample frame would be a list of all the students who go to Eastfield school.

To get a random sample of 100 students:

1) Give every student on the list a number.
2) Use random number tables, a calculator or a computer to get a list of 100 different random numbers between 1 and 2000.
3) The 100 students with those numbers would form your sample.

The Acid Test:

Learn everything on this page, then answer these questions.

You want to find out the average amount of pocket money received by students in your school.

1) Describe the population you're interested in.
2) What would your sample frame be?
3) How would you get a random sample of 50 from your population?

Systematic and Stratified Sampling

If you have a very large population, simple random sampling can be tricky to use.

Systematic Sampling — Choosing every n^{th} item

Higher

EXAMPLE: How would you get a systematic sample of 50 from a list of 2000 students at Eastfield Secondary School?

1) DIVIDE your population size by your sample size — 2000 ÷ 50 = 40.
2) Choose a RANDOM start number between 1 and 40 — let's say 3.
3) Your sample would be the third person on the list, then every 40th person after that until you have 50 people. So the sample would be the 3rd, 43rd, 83rd, 123rd, ... etc. students on the list.

Stratified Sampling — Representation for all Groups

Using STRATIFIED sampling can help you get a true picture (or REPRESENTATIVE sample) of a population. It's useful when your population's made up of groups (or categories) each containing members that are similar to each other in some way, e.g. age groups.

The number chosen from each group needs to be PROPORTIONAL to the size of the group in the population. Choose the right number from each group at random to make your sample.

EXAMPLE: The table shows the distribution of students in Years 9, 10 and 11 at Eastfield Secondary School. You want to choose a sample of 50 from the 1000 students.

	Boys	Girls	Total in Year
Year 9	179	221	400
Year 10	196	204	400
Year 11	119	81	200

With One Set of Categories...

(400 ÷ 1000) × 50 = 20 should be chosen at random from Year 9.
(400 ÷ 1000) × 50 = 20 from Year 10.
(200 ÷ 1000) × 50 = 10 from Year 11.

This should give a fairly representative sample — it's got the right proportion of students from each year group.

...or Two Sets of Categories

Higher

Now, you want the right proportions of boys and girls in each year group as well.

Of the 20 Year 9 students, (179 ÷ 400) × 20 = 8.95 should be boys.
Round this to 9 boys and 11 girls.

Of the 20 Year 10 students, (196 ÷ 400) × 20 = 9.8 should be boys.
Round this to 10 boys and 10 girls.

Of the 10 Year 11 students, (119 ÷ 200) × 10 = 5.95 should be boys.
Round this to 6 boys and 4 girls.

The Acid Test:

Learn everything on the page and make sure you understand it, then answer these questions.

1) How would you get a random sample of 30 from a population of 150 using systematic sampling?
2) A company has 10 managers, 22 middle managers and 68 shop-floor workers.
A representative committee of 10 employees is to be chosen using stratified random sampling.
How many of each type of employee would need to be in the sample?

Cluster and Quota Sampling

You need to know about three types of non-random sampling that are widely used.

Cluster Sampling — Cheaper than Random Sampling

Sometimes, in a large population, you get smaller groups called CLUSTERS.
These groups should be as similar as possible to each other.
For example, in a county the clusters could be towns or villages.

For cluster sampling:

1) first a random sample of CLUSTERS is chosen,
2) then a random sample is taken from each selected cluster.

EXAMPLE: If the government wanted to find out about spending habits in England, they would probably use cluster sampling. The clusters could be all the counties in England. A random sample of counties would be chosen and then a random sample of people within these counties would be surveyed.

It's easy to see that it would be cheaper for interviewers to just cover certain counties rather than the whole country.

Quota Sampling — Often used for Market Research

1) The population is divided up into groups based on AGE, GENDER and so on.
2) The interviewer will be told to interview a certain number of people from each group, e.g. 20 men and 20 women over the age of 40, 15 men and 15 women under 40.
3) This method of sampling is often used in interviews carried out on high streets, and the final choice of the sample members is down to the interviewer — it's not random.

Convenience Sampling — Just what it sounds like

The sample is chosen for convenience.
It's taken from a section of the population present at ONE PARTICULAR PLACE AND TIME.

These three types of sampling have the DISADVANTAGE of being NON-RANDOM, but they're CHEAP and EASY to use (see p.10 for advantages / disadvantages of sampling techniques).

The Acid Test:

Learn the three types of non-random sampling on this page, then cover the page and answer this question.

1) Say whether the samples used for these surveys are cluster, quota or convenience samples:
   a) For a transport survey, a county council chooses 100 postal districts at random from around the county. Twenty households from each postal district are then surveyed.
   b) A researcher uses a sample of 200 people on their way into Costcut supermarket between 9 a.m. and 10 a.m. in the morning.
   c) Paul surveys 200 people as they pass him in his local high street. He makes sure that 50 are women under the age of 30, 50 are men under the age of 30, 50 are women over the age of 30, and 50 are men over the age of 30.

Higher Higher Higher Higher Higher Higher Higher Higher

Strengths and Weaknesses of Sampling

Each sampling method has its own advantages and disadvantages. Here they are in detail. Make sure you know what each of the methods are before you read this page (see p.7-9).

1) **SIMPLE RANDOM SAMPLING**

Every member of the population has an **EQUAL CHANCE** of being selected, so a simple random sample is completely unbiased. But if the population is spread over a large area, whoever carries out the survey could have a lot of travelling to do.

2) **SYSTEMATIC SAMPLING**

This should produce an unbiased sample. Problems arise when the sample frame you use has some sort of **PATTERN**. For example if every tenth gizmo produced by a machine is faulty and you are sampling every tenth gizmo for quality control, your sample will either be completely faulty or completely without faults.
Either way, your sample is biased.

3) **STRATIFIED SAMPLING**

If you have **easy to define CATEGORIES** in the population (e.g. males and females) this is likely to give you a good sample. Stratified sampling isn't useful when there aren't any obvious categories or when the categories are hard to define.
It can be **EXPENSIVE** because of the extra detail involved.

4) **CLUSTER SAMPLING**

The main advantage of cluster sampling is that it saves on travel when the population is spread over a large area. It's easy to get a biased sample though — e.g. people living in the same postal district could have **SIMILAR INCOMES** or **EMPLOYMENT**.

5) **QUOTA SAMPLING**

This is **QUICK** to use and any member of the sample can be replaced by one with the same properties. If you have no sample frame (list of the population) — then the **ONLY** way of getting a sample may be quota sampling or convenience sampling.
Quota sampling can easily be biased, though — it's often used in street surveys by market research companies, so the sample chosen **DEPENDS ON THE INTERVIEWER**.
The people who refuse to take part may all have similar points of view on the topic being surveyed. For example if the survey was on working hours, those with the longest working hours might not have time to answer the questions.

6) **CONVENIENCE SAMPLING**

The convenience comes at a price — there's **NO ATTEMPT** to make the sample representative of the population being surveyed.

The Acid Test:

Learn the pros and cons of each of the 6 sampling methods, then answer this question.

1) In each case, say which sampling method is being used and state at least one advantage and one disadvantage of the method:
   a) The first 500 people to enter a multistorey car park are selected.
   b) Every tenth student is chosen from a school register.
   c) 1000 households are selected at random from a complete list of addresses in a city.

Higher Higher Higher Higher Higher Higher Higher Higher

Biased Samples

There are different ways that bias can creep in when you're sampling.
Here's a couple of them.

You need to Sample from the Right Population

It sounds obvious, but you need to be absolutely clear about what your population is when you're doing a statistical project. You'd be surprised how easy it is to get this wrong, and if you sample from the WRONG POPULATION, you'll introduce bias.

EXAMPLES OF SAMPLING FROM THE WRONG POPULATION:

1) A classic example is TELEPHONE POLLING. Say you want to find out about the eating habits of all the people in your town. You choose a sample selected at random from the phone book. The sample is biased — think about it. The population you're interested in is everyone who lives in the town, but your sample excludes anyone who isn't in the phone book (e.g. because they're ex-directory or don't have a phone).
2) A food company wants to find out about the snack preferences of young people in a city. They choose a random sample from all the students who go to a particular secondary school. The sample is biased because the population should be all the young people in the city, not just those that happen to go to that school.

You can get Bias if you choose a Non-Random Sample

How to be non-random:

1) Use cluster sampling
2) Use quota sampling
3) Use convenience sampling

(Pages 9 and 10 give you details on these, but you only need to know the details if you're doing *Higher*.)

EXAMPLES OF NON-RANDOM SAMPLING TECHNIQUES:

1) You want to find out if the students at your school think the tuck shop provides good value for money. You choose for your sample the first twenty people in the queue for the tuck shop at break time. You've got the population right — any student who goes to your school could (in theory) be in the queue. But the sample is non-random — people who think strongly that the tuck shop is bad value for money probably don't shop there. *For those of you doing Higher — this is convenience sampling.*
2) A car manufacturer sends out customer satisfaction questionnaires to all the people who've bought new cars from them in the past year. The sample of questionnaires they get back will be biased. People are more likely to return the questionnaire if they're really happy or really unhappy with the car — or have a lot of time on their hands.

The Acid Test:

Learn the different ways you can end up with biased samples then answer this question.

1) Say why these two samples are biased:
   a) For a science project, Jim wants to find out about the average size of fish in the Lake District. His sample consists of 100 fish caught in Windermere.
   b) A supermarket interviews all the people shopping there between 9 a.m. and 10 a.m. on a Saturday morning to get information about customer satisfaction.

Planning an Investigation

Use a Hypothesis to make things Clear

When you're planning an investigation you need to be clear about what it is you're trying to find out. So you need to have a RESEARCH QUESTION or HYPOTHESIS.
A hypothesis is a statement that you believe is true but that you haven't got evidence to support yet. Once you've got a hypothesis you'll know exactly what data to collect.

Examples of hypotheses:

1) Rick and Alex are playing a dice game. Rick is losing and thinks that since they're using Alex's dice, the dice must be loaded.
   — Rick's hypothesis is that the dice are biased.
2) Yvette thinks that students who watch a lot of television are less likely to do well in exams because they don't have as much spare time to study.
   — Yvette's hypothesis is that the more time a student spends watching television per week, the less well they do in examinations.

You can Break up your Research into Subquestions

In the examples above, each problem has just ONE question. If things are more complicated you'll have to break your investigation down into smaller chunks, called SUBQUESTIONS.

EXAMPLE: Breaking a question into subquestions

The Comfee furniture company is trying to work out a scale of charges for delivering sofas. They think the journey takes more time (and so will be more expensive) if the delivery address is further away from their storage depot.

The company's hypothesis is that the further a journey is, the longer it takes.

This is a really simple hypothesis, but it doesn't take into account the different types of road a delivery van has to travel on. A 200-mile journey down the motorway might be quicker than a 100-mile journey along country lanes.
So the company could break down their delivery areas into three categories:

1) Places that can be reached mainly by motorway.
2) Places that can be reached mainly by 'A' roads.
3) Other places.

They could then investigate each area separately.

The Acid Test:

Make sure you know what a hypothesis is.

Say what the hypothesis is for each of these situations:

1) The Yumyum sweet manufacturers claim that their chocolate bar is the UK people's favourite.
2) Pete thinks that Yumyums are cheating their customers by selling chocolate bars that are less than their stated weight of 70 grams.

More on Investigations

Once you've got a research question or hypothesis, you need to decide what data to collect. It has to be something that will provide evidence EITHER FOR OR AGAINST your hypothesis (it's no good having data that doesn't do either).

Next, choose HOW you're going to get the data. Here are four methods.

Questionnaires, Experiments, Raw or Secondary Data

1) **Questionnaires** — the data's collected by asking questions to members of the sample. The questions can take many different forms and you need to be really careful when you're designing a questionnaire. More on this later.
2) **Experiments** — instead of asking people questions, you could do an experiment, e.g. by measuring their height or how fast they can run. You have to use experiments to collect data on the natural world, such as heights of trees.
3) **Raw Data** — this is data that has been collected by someone else, but not processed in any way, for example census data.
4) **Secondary Data** — this is data that has been collected and processed for some other reason than the one you need to use it for. You need to take care when you use it, but it can still be handy. You can find secondary data in newspapers and magazines, on the internet, in databases and historical records, etc.

Choose the Best Method for Your Hypothesis

Some examples will make this clearer.

1) WARTSHIRE COUNTY COUNCIL'S HYPOTHESIS:
The people of Wartford travel less far to work than the people living in outlying villages.
The County Council would need to collect data on how far the people of Wartford and the outlying villages travel to work. A questionnaire would be a sensible way to do it.

2) MR PHITT THE P.E. TEACHER'S HYPOTHESIS:
Students who can run faster spend less money at the school tuck shop.
Mr Phitt could do an experiment to see how fast each student can run 100 metres, then get them to complete a questionnaire on how much they've spent at the tuck shop in the last month.

Higher

NOTE: In these two examples, these aren't the only ways of collecting data. In example 2 for instance, Mr Phitt could just ask the students if they can run fast — this mightn't be so accurate though. You need to be able to justify the method you choose and compare it with alternative methods.

Higher

The Acid Test:

Remember, you need to collect data that will either support or oppose your hypothesis.

Learn the four ways listed above to collect data, then turn over and write it all down.

Questionnaires

There's more to questionnaires than meets the eye — read on...

There are 3 Main Ways to do Questionnaires

1) FACE-TO-FACE interviews.
2) By POST.
3) TELEPHONE interviews.

These each have their ADVANTAGES and DISADVANTAGES.

1) If you interview face-to-face or by telephone, you're more likely to get responses than if people have to post their answers.
2) Also, you can ask more complicated questions, as you can explain what they mean to people who don't understand.

BUT... People are more likely to lie to you in a face-to-face interview, and when interviewing by telephone your sample will miss all the people without a telephone (among others).

Make Sure You Don't Collect Biased Data

There's five points to remember here:

1) Make sure you identify the population correctly (see pages 7 and 11).
2) Choose ways to distribute and collect your questionnaire that mean as large a proportion of your sample will respond as possible — keep it simple and easy.
3) Follow up people who don't respond to your questionnaire. Don't just forget about them.
4) Make your questionnaire as clear as possible, so people can record their answers accurately.
5) And lastly — don't lose any of your carefully collected data.

Questions Can Be Open or Closed

1) Closed questions have a FIXED NUMBER of possible answers — these could be yes/no or tick box questions.

EXAMPLES: Are you under 18 years of age?

Tick the mode of transport you use to get to school.
Bus ☐ Car ☐ Bicycle ☐ Walking ☐ Other ☐

The good thing about closed questions is that you can easily process the data collected. Also, if the question is well designed, the responses won't be AMBIGUOUS at all.

2) Open questions allow any answers.

EXAMPLE: What is your favourite TV program?

Open questions are particularly good in face-to-face interviews because you can follow up the answers. The problem is that you might end up with such a wide range of answers that the data is really hard to process.

The Acid Test:

Learn how to avoid collecting biased data from a questionnaire and the difference between open and closed questions.

1) Say whether each of these questions is open or closed:
a) Which is your favourite fish?
b) In which of the following would you prefer to live? a) the sea, b) mountains, c) a town.
c) Are you a dolphin?

Problems with Questions

Bad questions can make the best statistical investigation turn pear-shaped, and there's quite a few pitfalls to watch out for — you've got to be ready for them.

Design your Questionnaire Carefully

Bear these six points in mind when you design a questionnaire:

1) **MAKE SURE YOUR QUESTIONS ARE RELEVANT.**
   The data from the questionnaire should provide evidence either for or against your hypothesis. It's no good asking really fascinating questions if the answers aren't going to be useful.

2) **QUESTIONS SHOULD BE CLEAR AND EASY TO UNDERSTAND.**
   (your best bet is to assume that the people answering them are REALLY STUPID).

3) **ALLOW FOR ALL POSSIBLE ANSWERS TO YOUR QUESTION.**
   E.g. "What is your favourite subject — Maths, English or Science?" is difficult to answer truthfully if you like Art best.

4) **QUESTIONS SHOULDN'T BE LEADING.**
   Leading questions are ones that are more likely to get a certain answer.
   For example: "You do agree that thrash metal is really good music?"
   The problem with this question is that it could make the interviewee feel pressurised into saying 'yes'. A better question would be "*What type of music do you prefer to listen to?*"

5) **QUESTIONS SHOULD BE UNAMBIGUOUS.**
   Here's an example: "Do you play computer games a lot?"
   This question could be interpreted differently by different people. One person who plays 20 hours a week could answer yes, while another who plays the same amount could answer no. A better question would be "*How many hours do you play computer games per week?*"

6) **PEOPLE MAY NOT ANSWER QUESTIONS TRUTHFULLY.**
   This is often because they're embarrassed about the answer.
   For example: "Do you wear fashionable clothes?" (see next page for a way round this)

Test your Questionnaire with a Pilot Study

You should always use a PILOT STUDY to check for problems with your questionnaire. This is where you try the questionnaire out on a small group of people. The pilot study should help you spot any questions that are unclear or ambiguous, as well as any other unexpected problems.

After doing your pilot study, make sure you keep a RECORD of any problems that came up and the changes that you made to put them right.

The Acid Test:

LEARN the six points to bear in mind when designing a questionnaire. Close the book and write them from memory.

1) Give one criticism of each of these questions:
   a) Do you agree that maths is the most important subject taught in schools?
   b) Do you watch a lot of television?
   c) What is your favourite drink? Answer A, B or C. A) Tea B) Milk C) Coffee
   d) Are you a popular person who is easy to get on with?

Opinion Scales and Random Response

If you're doing Edexcel, you don't need the Opinion Scales bit — skip straight to Random Response.

Opinion Scales — Good for Getting More Detail

1) Opinion scales give you more information than yes/no questions.
2) The interviewee is given a statement and asked to use a scale of, say, 1 to 5, to say how strongly they agree or disagree with the statement.
3) The most commonly used scales are 1 to 5 or 1 to 10. But whatever scale you use, it's really important that the interviewee understands what the scale means.

EXAMPLE:

A sweet manufacturer wants to find out whether it would be worth introducing a chocolate bar with an orange centre. As part of their market research they want to find out if people like the combination of chocolate and orange.

They could use this question:

Do you like the flavours of chocolate and orange together? Yes/No

The problem is, this wouldn't show any difference between people who think the combination is just OK and the people who really love it and would buy loads of the chocolate.

It would be more useful to ask people to —

Circle the response that best describes how you feel about this statement, where 1 means strongly agree, 2 means agree, 3 means neutral, 4 means disagree and 5 means strongly disagree.

I like the flavours of chocolate and orange together. 1 2 3 4 5

Random Response — Useful for Sensitive Questions

You might need to ask a question that people may be EMBARRASSED to or not want to answer truthfully, such as, "*Have you committed a crime in the last 12 months?*"

The RANDOM RESPONSE technique is handy for reducing this problem.
Here's how you could use it to get more accurate data from the question above:

Toss a coin. If it lands on heads, tick the yes box; if it lands on tails, answer the question.
Have you committed a crime in the past 12 months? Yes No

If 100 people are surveyed you'd expect roughly 50 of them to toss heads and roughly 50 to toss tails. But if there are 60 ticks in the yes boxes, then it suggests that about 10 of the roughly 50 people who have tossed tails have commited a crime in the past 12 months. So it's likely that about 20 people in the sample of 100 have committed a crime in the past 12 months. The bigger your sample, the more accurate the results will be.

The interviewer doesn't know if a person ticked yes because they got 'heads' OR because they had committed a crime. This means the interviewee is more likely to answer the sensitive question truthfully (if you explain how the system works to them beforehand).

The Acid Test:

Make sure you understand what opinion scales are and how the random response technique works, then answer this question:

1) Design a question with an answer in the form of an opinion scale to find out how attractive the respondent finds a certain rock star.

Interviews

Instead of asking people to complete a written questionnaire, you can get data for your statistics project by doing interviews.

In Interviews You Question Each Person Individually

In interviews, you speak one-to-one with each person in your sample.

Question 154: Do you prefer dogs or antelopes?

An interview could be a questionnaire which you complete for the interviewee, or it could just be a list of topics which you want to find out their opinions on.

Interviews have pros and cons when compared to questionnaires.

MAKE SURE YOU KNOW WHAT THEY ARE:

Interviews Have Advantages...

1) You can ask more COMPLEX QUESTIONS in an interview.
   If someone doesn't understand the question, you're there to explain what it means.
2) Face-to-face interviews usually have a HIGHER RESPONSE RATE.
   A person asking you questions is a lot harder to ignore than a piece of paper.
3) You know the RIGHT PERSON answered the questions.
   If a questionnaire is sent out to the sample it's possible for anyone to fill it in.
   As a prank, children sometimes fill in questionnaires intended for their parents.
4) You can FOLLOW UP ANSWERS to questions if you think more information is needed.

...and Disadvantages

1) Interviews take A LONG TIME to carry out.
   Each interviewer can only talk to one person at a time.
   If you want to survey 100 people it'll take... well, ages.
2) Interviewing can be EXPENSIVE too.
   If you're running a market research company, employing interviewers will cost much more than sending out questionnaires.
3) The interviewees are more likely to LIE.
   People are much more likely to not tell the truth in a face-to-face interview if they're embarrassed about their answer.
4) It's hard to get information from a GEOGRAPHICALLY SPREAD OUT sample.
   If a sample included people living across a large area, it'd be very difficult to interview them all face-to-face. An interviewer would have a lot of travelling to do, whereas a questionnaire could just be mailed.
5) The answers could be recorded in a BIASED way.
   This could be by accident if the interviewer isn't very well trained, or deliberate if the interviewer has strong views on a subject.

The Acid Test:

Learn the ADVANTAGES and DISADVANTAGES of interviews — you'll need to know these.

1) Fred is an active member of the Stark Raving Bonkers Political Party.
   What is the disadvantage of using him as an interviewer to find out people's political views?

More on Obtaining Data

Statistical experiments measure how one variable changes when you change a second variable.

You need to Identify your Variables Clearly

It's important that you define your variables carefully. You need to control one variable and record its effect on another variable, while everything else should be kept constant:

1) The variable you're in control of is called the "EXPLANATORY" or "INDEPENDENT" variable.
2) The variable you then observe changes in is the "RESPONSE" or "DEPENDENT" variable.
3) On a graph, you always plot the explanatory variable on the horizontal (x) axis and the response variable on the vertical (y) axis.

EXAMPLE: A walker measures his pulse rate for different walking speeds. He graphs the data:

The explanatory variable is his walking speed, because he controls that. The speed he walks at affects his pulse rate (the response variable).
The faster he walks, the higher his pulse rate.

If he'd got his variables the wrong way round, this data would suggest that increasing his heart rate makes him walk faster — which doesn't make a lot of sense.

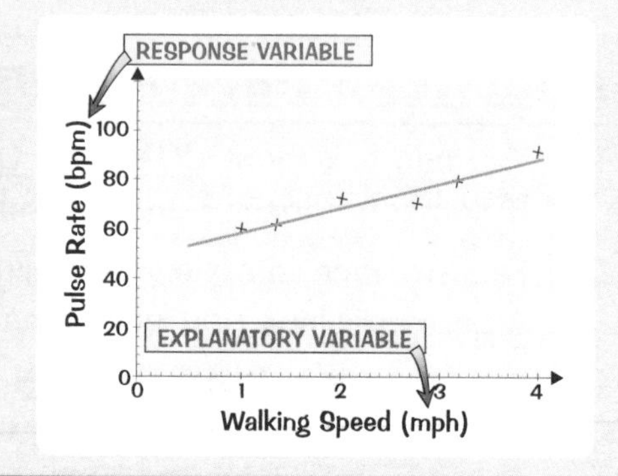

Design your Experiment Carefully — Keep it Fair

The walking experiment above would take some careful planning.
Some of the things the experimenter would need to think about are:

1) The walker needs to be walking at each of the different speeds for some time before measuring his pulse, so that his pulse has a chance to 'settle down' to the right value for that speed.
2) Any measuring devices need to be checked for accuracy and reliability.
3) Several measurements should be taken for each speed.
   Taking an average will increase the reliability of the results.

Keep all your Other Variables Constant

It's really important to keep any EXTRANEOUS VARIABLES (a mathsy term for any variables other than the two you're interested in) CONSTANT, so they don't influence the response variable. Then, any change in the response variable has to be due to changes in the explanatory variable.

Other variables which might have affected the walking experiment include:

1) WALKING SURFACE AND GRADIENT. All walking needs to be done on the same surface (e.g. tarmac, gravel, grass, etc.), and at the same gradient.
2) CONDITIONS. Changes in weather and wind direction can affect how difficult it is to walk. Since you can't actually control the weather, you just have to choose times to do the experiment when conditions are similar.
3) TIREDNESS. The walker's pulse rate should be back at rest rate before each trial. This means he's always starting from the same "zero" point.

Each of these must be kept as constant as possible, otherwise they might affect the results. They might even have more of an effect on the pulse rate than the walking speed.

More on Obtaining Data

It's Important to Identify all Extraneous Variables

It's not always possible to control all the variables in an experiment, but it's important that you realise what they all are — otherwise you could draw some invalid conclusions.

EXAMPLE: *100 individuals take part in an experiment over one year.*

The average number of hours they each slept per 24 hours was plotted against their age.

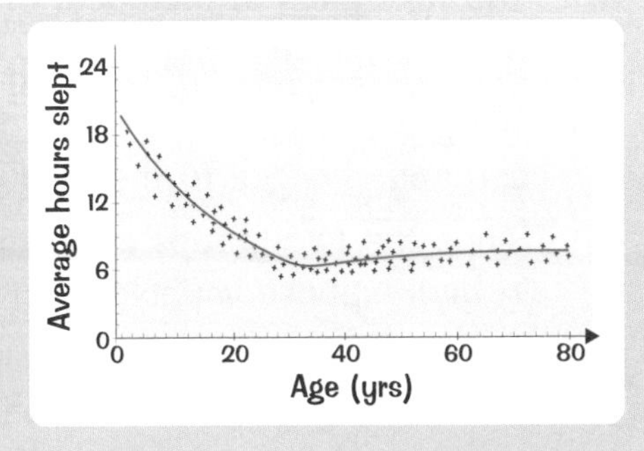

It would be very easy, from this data, to conclude that you need less sleep per day as you get older. But the situation is a bit more complicated than that.

You need to think about all the other factors that might have an influence on the length of time you sleep for. Stressful jobs or young families to look after can reduce the amount of sleep you get per night. Diet plays a significant role as well — for example, adults are likely to have much higher levels of caffeine in their diet than children, decreasing the number of hours they sleep for.

Control Groups make your Results Meaningful

A 'CONTROL GROUP' is a group that isn't part of the experiment, but is as similar to the experimental group as possible. You compare any changes in the experimental group with the control group. You can then tell whether the changes are due to your experiment or might have happened anyway.

EXAMPLE: A new drug is to be tested. 200 patients have volunteered. Design the experiment to carry out the testing.

1) First, you need to choose the people who are going to receive the drug, and the people in the control group. You need to select individuals for each group in a random way.
2) This can be done in several ways:
   You might use a random number table to decide.
   You could put patients' names in a hat and the first 100 names you pick out would go in the experimental group.
   A better way to do it would be to split the group of 200 in a similar way to taking a stratified sample (p.8). So, the experimental group and the control group should have approximately the same distributions of sex, age, ethnicity, etc. This is a better way of splitting up the group, because all these factors could affect how well the drug works.
3) The control group must be treated in the same way as the experimental group. This includes making them think they're getting treatment, even though they aren't really. The control group needs to be given a 'placebo' or 'dummy' medicine which won't have a physiological effect. This principal can be extended to diet, exercise routines, environment, etc.

The Acid Test:

Make sure you know how to SPOT AND CONTROL variables in your experiments.

1) Explain the purpose of a 'control group' in a statistical experiment. Describe how you would go about selecting a control group.
2) In designing an experiment you have already chosen an experiment group and a control group. What else do you have to bear in mind?

Matched Pairs & Before-and-After

Matched Pairs are Identical apart from the Test Variable

You can use 'MATCHED PAIRS' to investigate the effect of ONE factor alone.

1) You take pairs of members of your population who are alike in every way.
2) Put one member from each pair into each of two groups.
3) The groups are then treated differently in some way, and any changes to the response variable noted.
4) Since the two groups are similar in every way, any differences in the response variable must be due to the different treatment.

Identical twins are used a lot in matched pair studies by sociologists and psychologists.

EXAMPLE: *Tim wants to investigate the effects of two different soils on the fruit of a strawberry plant. He decides to do this using matched pairs.*

To make sure the two plants are identical in every way, Tim uses strawberry plants grown from cuttings off the same plant.

He puts the two young plants in pots containing the test soils, side by side in the greenhouse, and waits for the fruit to appear.

1) To make this a completely fair test, all extraneous variables need to be controlled. The two plants need to be kept at the same temperature, get the same amount of light and the same amount of water.
2) Since the only difference between the two plants will be the soil they've grown in, any differences in the size, colour or taste of the fruit will be due to the soil.

Before-and-After Experiments test the Same Group Twice

1) Like matched pairs, before-and-after experiments keep all but one factor constant.
2) For these experiments, the SAME GROUP of people (or things), are given a similar test before and after an event to see how they're affected by it.

EXAMPLE: A company that gives courses on improving your memory skills wants to test out a new system. Thirty volunteers are shown a list of twenty numbers and asked to write down as many as they can remember. After training in the memory system, the same group of people are given a similar test again.

If the system works, the results of the second test will be better than those of the first.

This sort of experiment has been used to test the effect of the long school summer holiday.

The Acid Test:

LEARN the similarities and differences between matched-pair and before-and-after experiments. Then answer this question.

1) Sharon wants to carry out an experiment to test the effect of light levels on a plant. She has two young pansies, grown from cuttings off the same plant. She puts one in a greenhouse and the other in a dark cellar. What is wrong with this experiment?

Capture / Recapture Method

Capture/recapture is a clever way to estimate the size of a constant population.

Both the Capture and Recapture need to be Random

EXAMPLE: Work out an estimate of the number of fish in a lake given the following information:

(i) A fisherman nets 50 fish from the lake. He marks all of them with a small tag and returns them alive to the lake.

(ii) A few days later another fisherman nets 60 fish. 15 of them are found to have been tagged by the first fisherman.

If you can assume that the sample of 60 fish is representative of the whole population, you can work out roughly how many fish there are in total.

Method 1 — Ratios

1) The ratio of tagged to untagged fish in the second net is 15:45 (which cancels to 1:3).
2) You know there are 50 tagged fish in the population.
3) So, multiply the ratio by 50 to get the total numbers of tagged and untagged fish:

   $(1 \times 50):(3 \times 50)$ or 50:150.

   So there are about 200 fish in the lake.

Method 2 — Fractions

1) The fraction of tagged fish in the second net will be the same as the fraction tagged in the whole lake.
2) Call the total population N.

So: $15/60 = 50/N$

$15N = 50 \times 60$

$N = 200$

BE VERY CAREFUL: *Capture/recapture only works in constant populations, i.e. the population has to made up of exactly the same members when the two samples are taken.*

It doesn't matter which method you use, so do the one you find easiest to remember. Remember to SHOW ALL YOUR WORKING though.

You Need to Make a Lot of Assumptions

You make a lot of ASSUMPTIONS when you use this method — so it's only an ESTIMATE.

1) You assume that the second net is perfectly representative of the whole population. For this to be true, the tagged fish will need to have had time (and opportunity) to fully mix back in with the rest of the population before the second sample is taken.
2) You have to assume that the capture and recapture are completely random. If the person doing the catching can see the tags, you could end up with a biased second sample.
3) You also assume the fish are unaffected by the first capture or the tagging/marking. They're returned alive and well, but some types of tag would make them easier to catch.

The Acid Test:

Learn all the details of the capture/recapture method for estimating population size.

1) Evelyn captures 30 frogs from her garden pond and carefully marks each before returning them to the water. The following day she captures 20 frogs and finds that 10 are marked. Estimate the number of frogs in Evelyn's pond.

Simulation

You can use random numbers to 'simulate' real random events (like rolling a dice).

Use Random Number Tables to Simulate Real Data

EXAMPLE: The table below contains random numbers. You can use it if you want to simulate the results of rolling a fair dice.

5712	2839	6210	5335	7691	7748	4452
5586	1784	7362	2731	1790	4283	5166
9000	8012	3502	7523	3450	3718	8926

Random number tables are usually much bigger than this one, and the individual values can have any number of digits.

There are loads of ways to do this using the table:

1) Probably the most obvious way is to read across each row and take the first digit of each number to be the result of a roll of the dice. You ignore any numbers with a first digit of 7 or more. The first 10 results using this method are: 5, 2, 6, 5, 4, 5, 1, 2, 1, 4. [Don't be tempted to read a 7 as a 1, an 8 as a 2, etc. If you do that, you've got more chance of generating a 1, 2 or 3 than a 4, 5 or 6 (1 = 1 or 7, 2 = 2 or 8, 3 = 3 or 9, 4 = 4 or 0)].
2) You could use the second, third or fourth digit of each random number instead, or read down the columns rather than across the rows. You could even use ALL the digits — reading left to right, right to left, diagonally, up and down and back up again...
3) However you choose to read the table, you need to make your method clear and stick to it.

You can use your Calculator to Generate Random Numbers

Your calculator will probably have a random number button. Look for "RAN" or "RAN#" (if you've got a graphical calculator, you might not have a RAN button — read the manual).

Chances are you'll have to press the 'Shift' or '2nd Fn' button first (on my calculator it's "shift •"), but it depends on the make of your calculator.

Calculators usually generate random numbers between 0 and 1 to 3 decimal places.
e.g. 0.693, 0.581, 0.002, 0.014, 0.088, 0.639

In the dice example above you might chose the last digit to simulate your roll score (ignoring 0, and anything above 6).

Albert wasn't so keen on the random thought generator

Or you can use a Computer

There are loads of different computer programs you can use to generate random numbers, but I'm just going to tell you how to do it in Excel — you can make yourself a random number table.

1) Open a new worksheet in Excel.
2) In cell A1, type =RAND() and press enter — this gives you a random number between 0 and 1 with loads of decimal places.
3) Copy and paste this into as many cells as you need.

The Acid Test:

Learn the three different methods on this page for getting random numbers, then answer this question.

1) Use your calculator to generate twenty random two-digit numbers. Explain your method clearly.

Revision Summary for Section One

Phew — that was a bit of a monster of a first section, but there's loads of useful stuff in there. It'll come in handy wherever you are... well, particularly if you're in a Statistics Exam. Use these questions to test what you know, and what you don't. Keep practising them till you can get them all right without looking back at the section. Go on — you know you want to.

Keep learning the basic facts until you know them

1) Define "primary data" and give three possible sources of it.
2) Define secondary data. What things do you have to be sure of before you use a source of secondary data for a statistical project?
3) Define qualitative and quantitative data.
4) What is the difference between discrete and continuous data? Give one example of each.
5) Give a definition and an example for each of the following:
   a) categorical scale, b) rank scale, c) interval scale, d) ratio scale.
6) What is bivariate data?
7) What does the word "census" mean?
8) Give an example of a population that it wouldn't be practical to take a census of.
9) Describe how to take a simple random sample of 25 from a population of 5000.
10) Describe how to take a systematic sample of 25 from a population of 5000.
11) What is a stratified sample? Give a method for taking one.
12) List three non-random sampling methods.
    Give one advantage and one disadvantage of each of these methods.
13) Describe two causes of bias when you're taking a sample.
14) What is a hypothesis, and why do you need one?
15) Give three different ways to carry out questionnaire surveys.
16) What can you do to reduce the chances of collecting biased data from a questionnaire?
17) List three things you need to bear in mind when designing each question in a questionnaire.
    What's the best way to test the quality of a questionnaire once you've written it?
18) What is an opinion scale?
19) What's the advantage of using an opinion scale instead of a simple "yes/no" question?
20) Describe the method of random response questioning.
    What sort of question would random response be suitable for?
21) Give four advantages and four disadvantages of carrying out face-to-face interviews rather than asking your sample to fill out a paper questionnaire.
22) Explain the "explanatory variable" and "response variable" in the context of statistical experiments.
23) Why do you need to keep all other variables apart from the explanatory and response variables constant during experiments?
24) What is a control group?
25) What are matched pairs?
26) Explain the process of capture/recapture for estimating populations.
27) What condition <u>needs</u> to be true of the population for you to be able to use capture/recapture?
28) What assumptions do you make when you use capture/recapture?
29) How might you use random number tables to simulate the results of tossing a fair coin?
30) Explain how you can generate random numbers on your calculator.

Frequency Tables

Frequency tables can be done either in columns or rows, and let you see lots of raw data more easily.

Frequency Tables Contain Raw Data

1) The word FREQUENCY just means how many, so a FREQUENCY TABLE is just a "How many in each group" table.
2) All frequency tables have 3 columns (or 3 rows).
3) The first column (or row) just gives the GROUP LABELS — the different categories (e.g. 1 goal, 2 goals, etc.)
4) The second column (or row) gives the ACTUAL DATA — in the form of a TALLY.
5) The last column (or row) is the FREQUENCY, which you get by adding up the tally marks.

EXAMPLE: *A hockey team lists the number of goals they score in each match of a season. Draw a frequency table for the data.*

1, 2, 0, 3, 2, 1, 0, 2, 3, 2, 2, 1, 2, 0, 1, 5.

Goals	Tally	Frequency
0					3
1						4
2	~~				~~		6
3				2
4		0
5			1

Total: 16

Draw a little tally mark in the right row to represent each piece of data.

Tallies are "bunched" together in fives, i.e. ~~||||~~ = 5

It's a good idea to cross off your data as you put the tally marks into the table, e.g. ~~1~~, ~~2~~, ~~0~~, 3... that way you know you haven't missed one or counted one twice.

Add up the frequency column to make sure it equals the number of games (or whatever).

Don't be clever and just fill in the frequency column by sight without doing the tally column. You'll just end up making mistakes that way.

You can Draw Frequency Tables Horizontally or Vertically

This table is the same as the top one, just turned around — easy.

Goals	0	1	2	3	4	5
Tally	|||	||||	~~||||~~		||			
Frequency	3	4	6	2	0	1

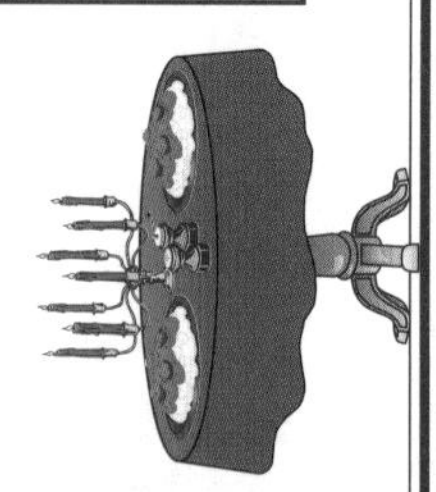

The Acid Test:

Learn how to put together a frequency table, then turn over and write it all down.

1) Alan records the number of coins in his pocket at the end of each day in June. Construct a frequency table to show the results.
5, 4, 3, 2, 3, 4, 4, 2, 0, 3, 4, 5, 4, 1, 3, 4, 2, 3, 2, 4, 3, 1, 2, 2, 3, 4, 2, 3, 5, 4.

Grouped Frequency Tables

Grouped frequency tables split data into groups using class intervals.

Use Grouped Frequency Tables When you've got Lots of Data

You often use GROUPED FREQUENCY TABLES when you've got too many pieces of data to think about individually, or when they are all different.

EXAMPLE: Amanda recorded the number of runs she scored in 12 school cricket matches:
10, 1, 9, 5, 8, 6, 15, 5, 12, 5, 16, 0

Runs	0 – 4	5 – 9	10 – 14	15 – 20
Tally	||	||||̶ |	||	||
Frequency	2	6	2	2

Here, there are gaps between each upper class limit and the next lower class limit (e.g. the first class ends at 4 and the second class starts at 5). That's because the data's discrete (see p.2), so nothing comes between 4 and 5, etc.

Be Careful with Class Intervals for Continuous Data

If you've got continuous data, you can use INEQUALITIES to define your class intervals.

Remember that:

$>$ means "Greater than"	$\geq$ means "Greater than or equal to"
$<$ means "Less than"	$\leq$ means "Less than or equal to"

EXAMPLE: *Adam measured the heights of 12 plants in a biology experiment to the nearest 0.1 cm. Here are his results:*
6.2, 1.3, 5.0, 7.2, 3.1, 8.8, 13.7, 7.1, 4.9, 19.6, 10.0, 15.0

1) First, choose the CLASS WIDTHS (unless you're told what to use). What class widths you choose depends on how detailed you want your table to be (see p.27).
2) Using inequalities, define your class intervals. Every possible value needs a group to go into:

Height	$0 \leq h < 5$	$5 \leq h < 10$	$10 \leq h < 15$	$15 \leq h < 20$
Tally	|||	||||̶	||	||
Frequency	3	5	2	2

So, 5.0 would go in the 2nd group, and anything less than 5.0 would go in the 1st group.

3) Remember when you're using tables like this, that they're only as ACCURATE as the original data. E.g. if you measured the heights of the plants to the nearest 0.01 cm, you might find the plant you thought was 5.0 cm tall was actually only 4.97 cm tall. That would put it in the first group, NOT the second.

The Acid Test:

Learn all the details on this page, then turn over and write down everything you've learned. Good clean fun.

1) Using the data on the heights of the 12 plants above, complete a grouped frequency table using the following class intervals:
$0 < h \leq 5$ $5 < h \leq 10$ $10 < h \leq 15$ $15 < h \leq 20$

Simplifying and Analysing Data

Having lots of data is all well and good, but big complicated tables are really hard to analyse. Simplifying tables makes them easier to get your head round, but you do lose detail in the process.

Whenever you SIMPLIFY tables of data, you're likely to end up with LESS INFORMATION in the new table than you started with (not surprising really).

You need to know the different ways of simplifying tables, as well as HOW and WHY simplifying affects the usefulness of your data.

EXAMPLE: *Number of criminal events involving firearms reported in Scotland by year.*

Weapon	1992	1993	1994	1995	1996
Shotgun	257	255	195	140	91
Rifle	11	11	13	19	15
Pistol	39	50	72	75	186
Air weapon	1159	1036	1005	1139	1060
Imitation gun	152	87	137	104	133
Other	341	334	366	244	164

There's a lot of information in this table, which makes it very difficult to spot trends (general patterns in the data).

The Easiest Way of Simplifying is Totalling

If you TOTAL THE DATA FOR EACH YEAR you get:

Total number of criminal events involving firearms in Scotland by year.

Year	1992	1993	1994	1995	1996
Total	1959	1773	1788	1721	1649

This new table is much easier to form useful conclusions from.

1) The trend seems to be that gun crime is generally DECREASING.
2) It's useful to look at any bits of the data that DON'T follow the general trend as well. So, between 1993 and 1994, there was actually a slight increase in reported gun crime. But look at the year before that — there had been a huge drop between 1992 and 1993.
3) You could go on to compare the data with earlier and later years, or crime rates in other regions, if you had similar data for them.

DISADVANTAGES OF TOTALLING:

1) You've lost all the DETAIL about INDIVIDUAL weapon types.
2) Whilst you can see the overall crime decreasing, look at the 'pistols' row in the original table — it seems to be increasing dramatically. Facts like this one are LOST by totalling.

Simplifying and Analysing Data

You Can Work Out Percentages

You can look at changes in the proportion of crimes carried out using each type of weapon by calculating PERCENTAGES. Just looking at 1995 and 1996:

Weapon	1995	1996
Shotgun	8.1%	5.5%
Rifle	1.1%	0.9%
Pistol	4.4%	11.3%
Air weapon	66.2%	64.3%
Imitation gun	6.0%	8.1%
Other	14.2%	9.9%

Percentage breakdown by weapon type of all reported gun crimes in Scotland – 1995/1996.

1) This table lets you look at the PROPORTION of each year's gun crime by weapon type.
2) Clearly the proportion of gun crime using 'pistols' is greater in 1996 than 1995, and the percentage of gun crime using bigger guns is down a bit.
3) The proportion using air weapons has stayed relatively steady, and is by far the highest.

DISADVANTAGES OF PERCENTAGE BREAKDOWN TABLES:

1) We don't know from this table whether TOTAL CRIME has increased from one year to the next.
2) Nor do we know HOW MANY CRIMES there were of each type.

A COMBINATION of the two different tables gives you a good overview of the data.

Simplify Data by Grouping it

If you have lots of data that's all DIFFERENT, it can help to put it in a GROUPED FREQUENCY TABLE. You have to be very careful not to DISTORT your data when you choose your class intervals.

EXAMPLE: *A 100 m sprinter records the following practice times (in seconds):*

11.56, 10.47, 10.03, 10.94, 11.89, 11.62, 10.81, 11.77, 10.20, 11.91, 10.55

He records them, accurate to 0.1 seconds, in a grouped frequency table:

Time (s)	Frequency
$9.0 < t \le 9.5$	0
$9.5 < t \le 10.0$	1
$10.0 < t \le 10.5$	2
$10.5 < t \le 11.0$	3
$11.0 < t \le 11.5$	0
$11.5 < t \le 12.0$	5

The data's much easier to handle in this format, but the way he's put the table together is a bit MISLEADING. By reducing the number of SIGNIFICANT FIGURES of his measurement, the sprinter has distorted his data.

His fastest time was actually 10.03 seconds. He rounded this to 10.0 and counted it in the $9.5 < t \le 10.0$ group. This suggests he broke the 10 second barrier, which he didn't.

...the sprinter (Bob) decides to simplify his table even further...

Simplifying and Analysing Data

Higher

Combining Class Intervals gives you a Simpler Table

You can simplify a grouped frequency table by COMBINING CLASSES.

Bob, the sprinter, decides to simplify his table (see p.27) by halving the number of classes.

Time (s)	Frequency
$9.0 < t \leq 10.0$	1
$10.0 < t \leq 11.0$	5
$11.0 < t \leq 12.0$	5

ADVANTAGE:

1) The new table is much smaller and simpler to look at.

DISADVANTAGES:

1) IMPORTANT DETAILS have been lost.
For example, the second and third groups (10-11 and 11-12) now have the same frequencies. This masks the fact that most of his times were either really slow or quite fast. There was a big gap in the original data between 11 and 11.5 seconds.
2) The 9-10 second group is completely unnecessary. Using the original data, none of Bob's times would actually go in it. It just distorts the data even further than the first table did. (It might also be worth noticing that most of this group is well below the Olympic 100 m record — hmmm...)

Learn to look for TRENDS in data, but be careful not to oversimplify the situation.

The Acid Test:

Learn everything from these three pages. Make sure you know the advantages and disadvantages of simplifying tables.

1) The table shows the number of people in different professions caught speeding over the years 1995 to 1999:

a) Draw another table to show the total number caught speeding in each year.
b) What trends does this new table show?
c) What information is lost in this new table?
d) Do a percentage breakdown by profession of people caught speeding between 1995 and '99.
e) What are the advantages and disadvantages of the percentage breakdown?

Professions	1995	1996	1997	1998	1999
Teachers	18	32	48	72	84
Lawyers	40	46	53	59	63
Editors	27	36	42	64	78
Lumberjacks	23	19	16	12	10

2) The following times were recorded, in seconds, in the world championship snail racing competition:
15.25, 15.04, 15.73, 16.42, 16.94, 15.85, 16.96, 15.02, 15.89, 16.53, 16.74, 15.94

a) Record them, accurate to 0.1 seconds, in a grouped frequency table, with six equal classes between 14 and 17 seconds.
b) How has the data been distorted?
c) If you halve the number of classes, what details are lost?

Contestant 13 was disqualified due to a technicality

Bar and Pie Charts

There are several different ways of drawing bar charts and pie charts. The basic stuff on bar and pie charts is covered in "normal" maths, so I'm only going to talk about the more interesting stuff.

Pictograms use Pictures to Represent Data

EXAMPLE: *A council employee did a survey of customer satisfaction on the buses by questioning passengers on a Saturday afternoon. 70 people were happy with the service, but 50 people thought it wasn't good enough. A similar survey was also done the following afternoon. On this occasion there were 160 people who said 'good' and 80 who said 'bad'.*

The pictogram on the right shows this data.

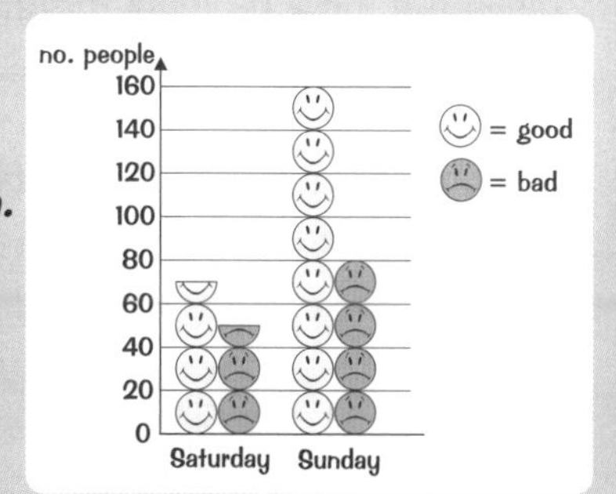

Another way of showing the data is in terms of percentages:

percentage 'good' $= \frac{70}{70+50} = 58.3\%$

Saturday

Sunday

0%

100%

percentage 'good' $= \frac{160}{160+80} = 66.7\%$

This chart shows that a **HIGHER PROPORTION** of those passengers questioned on Sunday were happy with the service than those questioned on Saturday.

Higher

Comparative Pie Charts use Areas

COMPARATIVE PIE CHARTS use the same area for each unit of data.

The council employee decides to put Saturday's data into a pie chart with a radius of 1.4 cm.

Working out the angles is fairly easy:

Total number of people interviewed = 120

Good = 70, so angle = (70/120) × 360 = 210°

Bad = 50, so angle = (50/120) × 360 = 150°

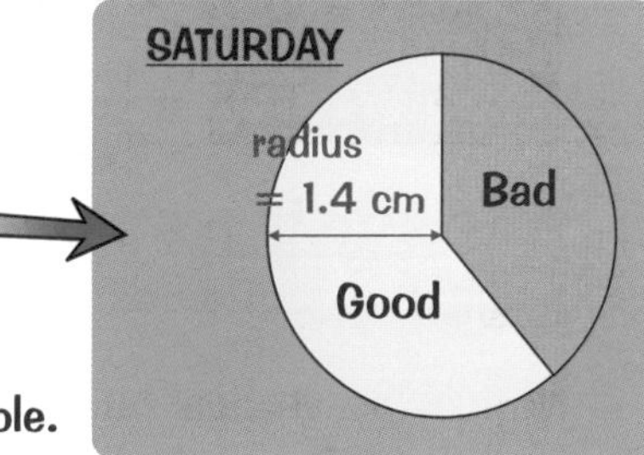

Now he wants a comparative pie chart for Sunday's data.

Saturday's chart has a radius of 1.4 cm and represents 120 people.

So: area for 120 people $= \pi r^2 = 1.4^2\pi$ cm^2

area for 1 person = 0.052 cm^2.

Use this to work out the radius of the other pie chart:

Sunday's survey had 240 people. 1 person = 0.052 cm^2, so

area for 240 people = 240 × 0.052 = 12.48 cm^2.

Work out its radius:

area $= \pi r^2$, so radius $= \sqrt{(\text{area}/\pi)} = \sqrt{12.48/\pi} =$ 1.99 cm = 2 cm

Finally, work out the angles...

Good = (160/240) × 360 = 240°

Bad = (80/240) × 360 = 120° ...and draw the pie chart.

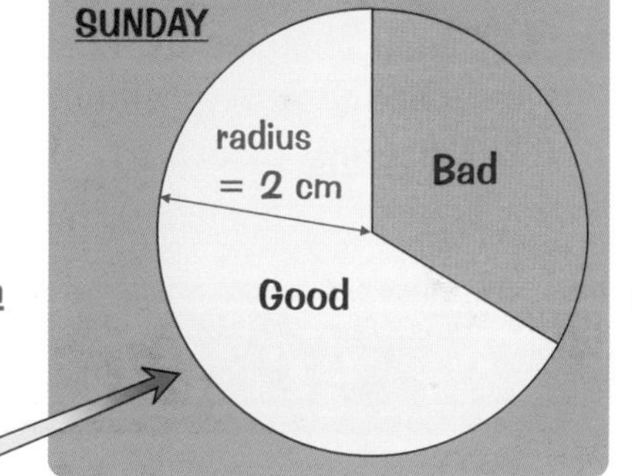

The Acid Test:

1) Draw comparative pie charts from this data. Use a radius of 2 cm for New Zealand.

Manchester Commonwealth Games 2002 Medals	Gold	Silver	Bronze
Australia	82	62	62
New Zealand	11	13	21

Discrete Data and Step Polygons

Graphs of discrete data look different from graphs of continuous data — and you need to be experts at both types. The discrete graphs on this page use vertical lines and steps.

A Line Graph is a bit like a Bar Chart — but with Lines

These are used to show frequency distributions for DISCRETE data.

Example: *Boxes of matches claim to have an average content of 48 matches. George counts the exact number of matches in each of 10 boxes. The frequency table and line graph below show her results.*

Matches	46	47	48	49	50
Frequency	0	2	5	2	1

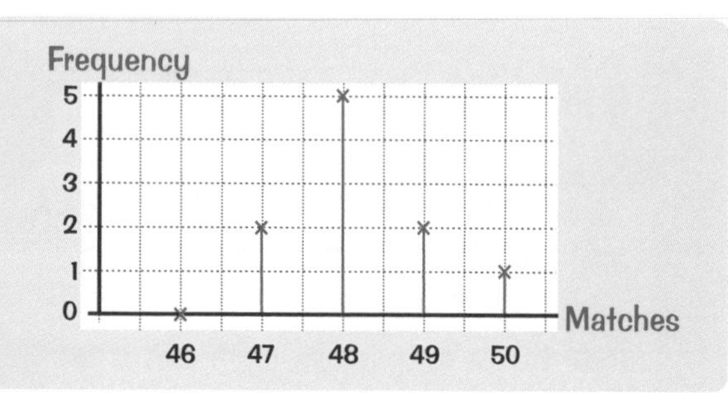

Cumulative Frequency Step Polygons

CUMULATIVE FREQUENCY is just a 'running total' of the frequencies.
Using the matches example from above:

1) Make a THIRD ROW in the table for the cumulative frequency — this is the RUNNING TOTAL of the second row.

Matches	46	47	48	49	50
Frequency	0	2	5	2	1
Cumulative Frequency	0	0 + 2 = 2	2 + 5 = 7	7 + 2 = 9	9 + 1 = 10

2 + 2 = 4

That's right... it's a *running total*. And the prize for the corniest joke in CGP history goes to...

2) For DISCRETE DATA, the cumulative frequency polygon is plotted as a STEP GRAPH like this:

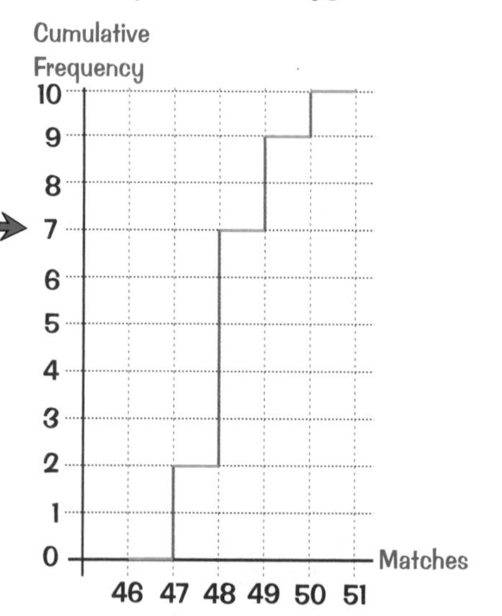

Notice the vertical bits (the purple lines) are the same height as the vertical lines in the first graph above.

You get flat steps because the cumulative frequency only changes at 47, 48, 49 and 50. It doesn't change at any other points, because the data is discrete (see p.2).

Higher Higher Higher Higher

The Acid Test:

Learn the two different types of graph above, then cover up the page and answer this question.

1) Amanda rolls a dice 20 times and records the results in a frequency table:

Score	1	2	3	4	5	6
Frequency	3	3	2	6	4	2

Draw a line graph and a cumulative frequency step polygon for this data.

Other Diagram Types

When your data's continuous, you draw polygons and curves instead of steps.

I'm going to use the example on plant heights from p.25 to demonstrate — Adam came up with this table:

Height	$0 \le h < 5$	$5 \le h < 10$	$10 \le h < 15$	$15 \le h < 20$
Frequency	3	5	2	2

A Frequency Polygon Uses the Midpoint of Each Class

1) You need to work out the MIDPOINTS for each class of heights first:

Height	$0 \le h < 5$	$5 \le h < 10$	$10 \le h < 15$	$15 \le h < 20$
Midpoint	2.5	7.5	12.5	17.5
Frequency	3	5	2	2

2) Then PLOT the frequency polygon:

Plot the midpoint of each class against its corresponding frequency.

Because it's a polygon (rather than a curve), you join the points with straight lines.

(The straight lines just mean you're assuming the data's evenly spread in each interval — but you don't need to worry about that.)

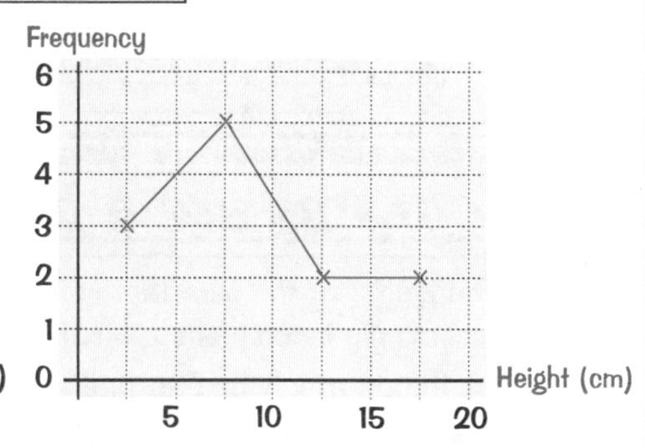

You can Plot Cumulative Frequency Polygons

The CUMULATIVE FREQUENCY is the 'running total' of heights (or whatever) — see p.30. You plot the cumulative frequency against the HIGHEST VALUE in each class. That's because this data can only tell you for sure how many plants are less than a certain height.

Height	$0 \le h < 5$	$5 \le h < 10$	$10 \le h < 15$	$15 \le h < 20$
Plot at height	5	10	15	20
Cumulative frequency	3	8	10	12

1) The points in a cumulative frequency polygon are joined with straight lines.
2) You might be asked to draw a 'cumulative frequency curve' instead. Then you need to draw a smooth curve through the points.
3) If you're just asked for a 'cumulative frequency diagram', you can draw either.

(If you're interested — you can draw either, because they both work for continuous data. Which one you draw depends on what assumptions you're making about the distribution of the data.)

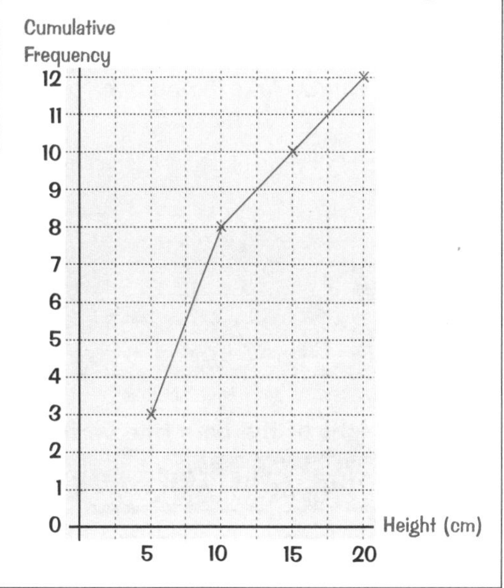

The Acid Test:

1) Convert this frequency polygon into a cumulative frequency polygon.

Grouped frequency polygon to show pupils' marks in Yr 11 English test.

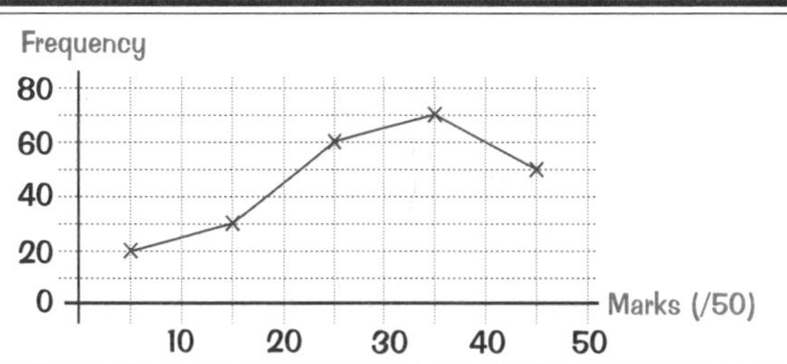

Other Diagram Types

These two are both based on bar charts.

Population Pyramids are made of Bar Charts

Population pyramids consist of TWO bar charts side by side to contrast two lots of information.

EXAMPLE: The students at St Thomas' (a specialist college for Mathematical Certainty) who gained a gold certificate in this year's Maths Challenge competition have been split up by gender and age in the table below. Draw a population pyramid to show this data.

Age in complete years	Boys (%)	Girls (%)
16-17	25	10
14-15	15	30
12-13	10	10

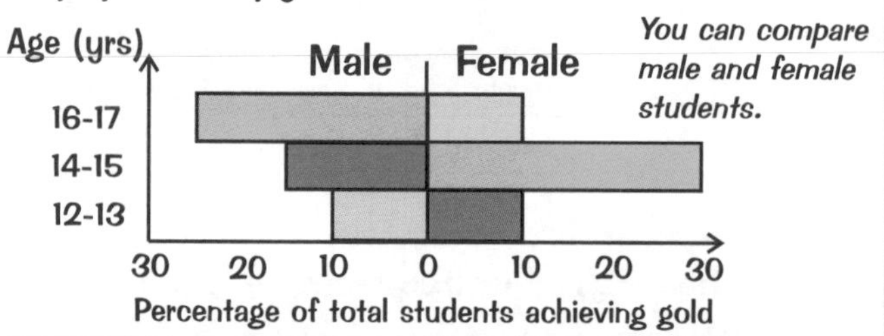

You can compare male and female students.

Histograms are a bit like Bar Charts — but Not

It's not the height of the bars that counts — it's the area. So, instead of nice easy-to-understand bar charts you get seemingly incomprehensible monsters, and yes, that makes them a firm favourite with the Examiners.

In fact things aren't half as bad as that — but only if you LEARN THE THREE RULES:

1) It's not the height, but the AREA of the bar that represents the frequency.
2) Work out what frequency is represented by EACH UNIT OF AREA (e.g. each cm^2).
3) Find the AREA (e.g. in cm^2) of each bar, and so work out the frequency represented by each bar.

EXAMPLE:
The histogram below represents the age distribution of people arrested for slurping boiled sweets in public places in 1995. Given that there were 36 people in the 55 to 65 age range, find the number of people arrested in all the other age ranges.

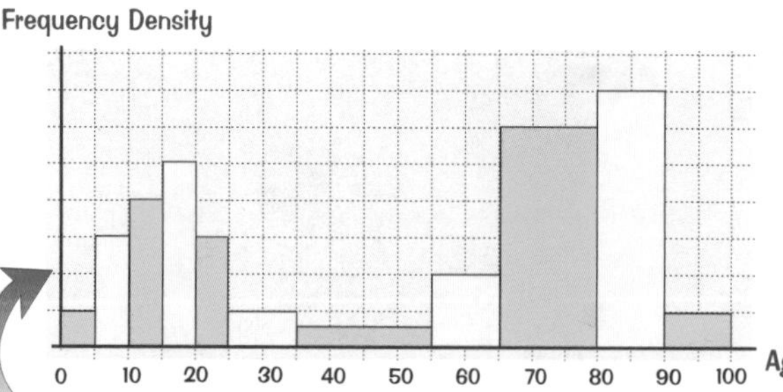

ANSWER: The 55-65 bar represents *36 people* and contains *4 dotted squares*, so *each dotted square* must represent *9 people*.

The rest is easy. E.g. the 80-90 group has 14 dotted squares so that represents $14 \times 9 =$ *126 people*.

The height of the bars (the vertical axis) is called the frequency density...

FREQUENCY DENSITY = FREQUENCY ÷ CLASS WIDTH

The *class width* is the width of the bar on the x-axis.

Use this formula to work out how high each bar should be when you're drawing a histogram.

E.g. say you've got a grouped frequency distribution with a frequency of 40 in the $5 < x \leq 10$ class — your frequency is 40, your class width is 5, so your bar needs to be 8 units high.

The Acid Test:

LEARN the THREE RULES for Histograms and the formula for frequency density. Turn over and write it all down.

1) Jo makes 15 calls of up to 5 minutes long, 20 calls between 5 and 15 minutes and 15 calls between 15 and 30 minutes. Using these intervals, draw a histogram to show the information.

Stem & Leaf Diagrams and Shading Maps

These diagrams are really easy to do. You've only got one or two things to remember....

Stem and Leaf Diagrams Show Shapes of Distributions

EXAMPLE: The ages of the members of a 'seniors' yoga class are listed below.

81, 70, 67, 56, 59, 51, 64, 73, 62, 71, 64, 64. Draw a stem and leaf diagram of this data.

1) First decide on the 'stem' for your diagram.

The stem is often the first digit of the numbers — so we'll use the TENS digit in this example.

5 |
6 |
7 |
8 |

2) Add the UNITS of each number one by one from the list. DON'T MISS ANY OUT.

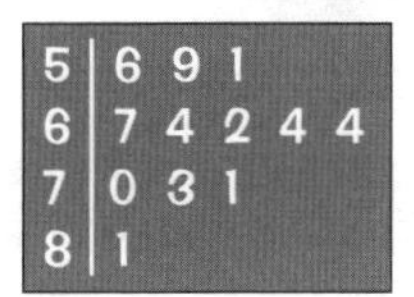

3) Then sort the leaves into order and add a KEY:

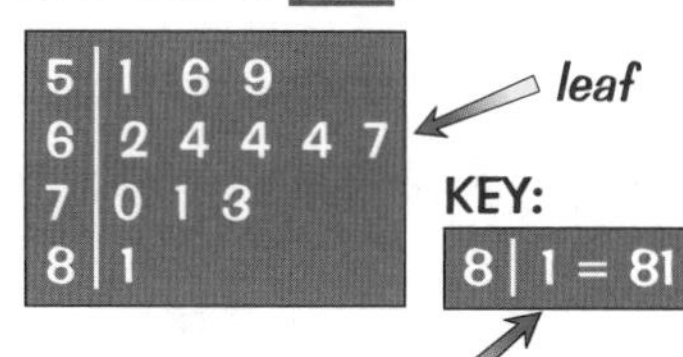

Your diagram must have a key. If you forget the key, you'll lose marks.

You can Compare Two Sets of Data Back-to-Back

The ages of a second yoga class can be added back-to-back to the first stem and leaf diagram. This keeps the data for each yoga class separate.

It then looks like this:

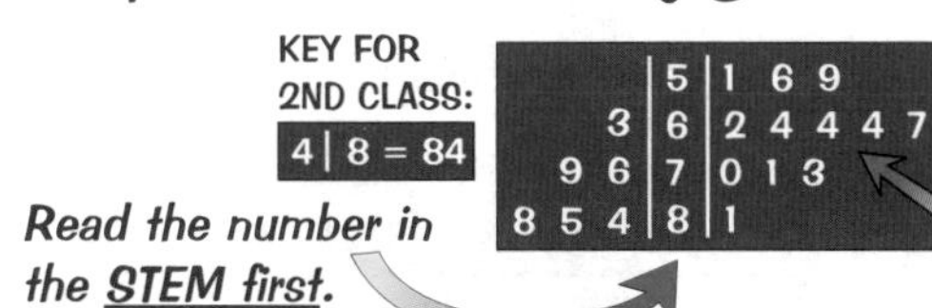

Read the number in the STEM first.

The MODAL (most common) age is 64. The 4s being side by side sort of stand out.

You can see that this second group are generally older.

You can also work out the range for each yoga class — you can easily see the smallest and largest ages for each class. E.g. the range of the second class is 88 – 63 = 25 years.

Choropleth Maps use Shading, Hatched Lines or Dots

1) Different REGIONS of the map are shaded differently — the DARKER the shading (or closer together the hatching or dots), the HIGHER the value of the data for that region.
2) You get a KEY with a choropleth map that tells you what each type of shading means.
3) You'll be expected to be able to 'READ' a map using the key, SHADE simple maps using data from a table and make CONNECTIONS between two different maps (e.g. a choropleth map of population density and a road map).

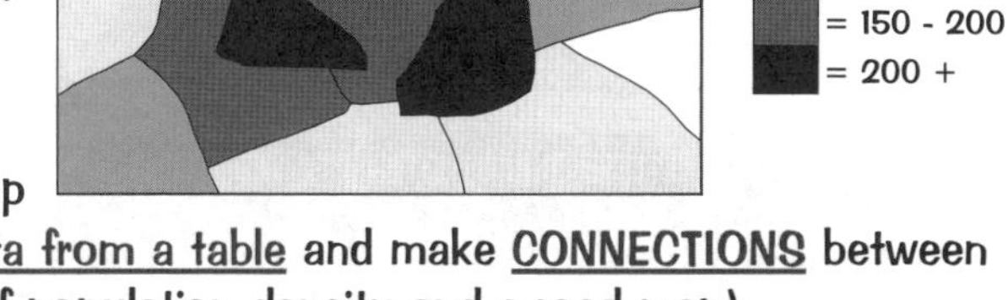

...it all sounds a bit 'Geography' to me.

The Acid Test:

STEM and LEAF diagrams won't make you a great biologist, but they will get you a few easy marks in the maths exam.

1) The commuting distances of various people to two cities are given below in miles:

City 1: 26, 23, 18, 39, 13, 27, 12, 28, 18, 36, 14, 41 City 2: 16, 27, 32, 44, 18, 33, 26, 42, 28, 32, 37, 32

a) Draw one stem and leaf diagram to show all the data.
b) What are the modal distances for each city?
c) What are the commuting ranges for the two cities?
d) To which city do commuters generally travel further?

Transforming Data

Sometimes you have to 'transform' (change) the way you show data.
There are lots of possibilities, but here are the common ones.

Change a Bar Chart to a Pie Chart in a few steps

EXAMPLE:

Show the information in this bar chart on a pie chart:

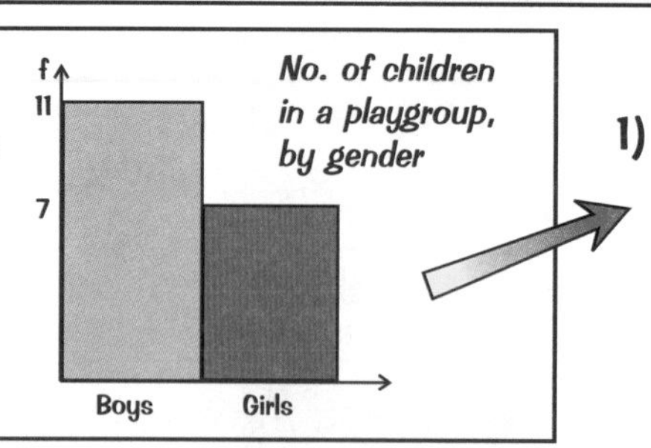

1) You need to figure out the TOTAL number of CHILDREN:

TOTAL = 11 + 7 = 18

2) Now you can work out the ANGLES for your pie chart:

18 people = 360°

Therefore 1 PERSON = 360° / 18 = 20°

So 11 boys = 11 × 20° = 220°

And 7 girls = 7 × 20° = 140°

Hint: Check angles add up to 360°: 220° + 140° = 360°

3) Then just draw your pie chart. You'll probably be told what radius to use:

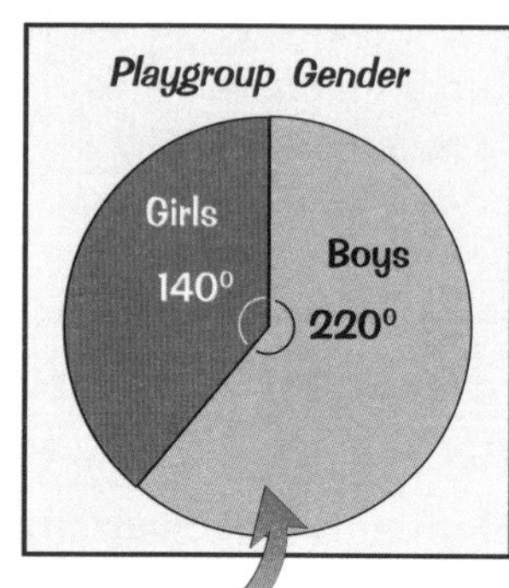

Use Pie Chart Angles to draw a Bar Chart

EXAMPLE: 240 Year 10 pupils are split into three groups by attendance — 'almost always attend', 'usually attend', and 'rarely attend'. Using this pie chart, construct a comparative bar chart.

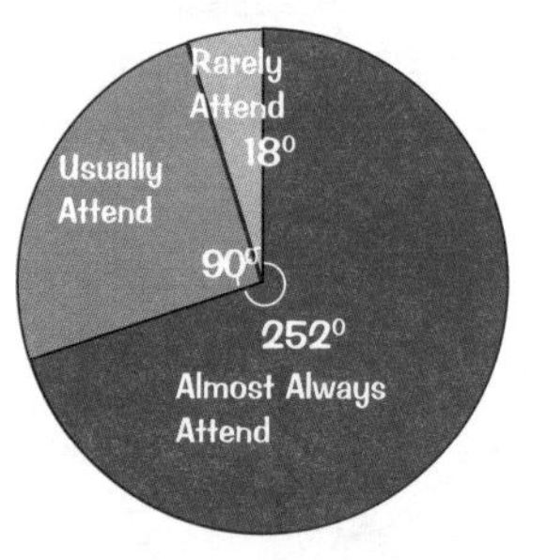

Year 10 Attendance

1) First of all measure the angles: You get 252°, 90°, and 18°.

2) You then work out the PERCENTAGE each angle equals:

252° / 360° × 100 = 70%

90° / 360° × 100 = 25%

18° / 360° × 100 = 5%

3) Now change the percentages to actual numbers in each category.

You know there are 240 Yr 10 pupils:

5% of 240 = 12 rarely attend

25% of 240 = 60 usually attend

70% of 240 = 168 almost always attend

4) Finally, draw the bar chart:

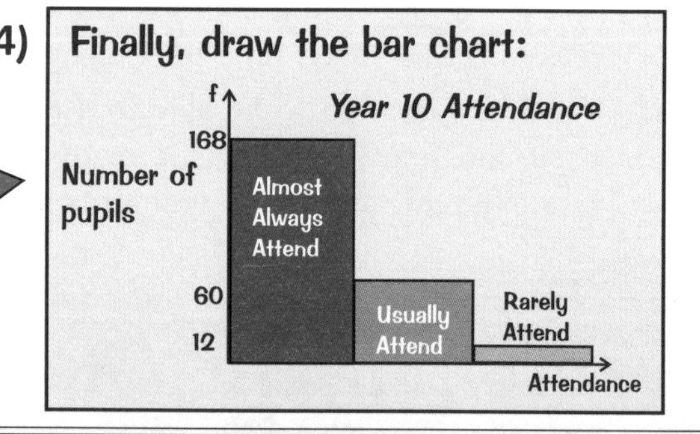

The Acid Test:

LEARN how to change a BAR CHART to a PIE CHART and back again until you feel sick — then go and eat a pie.

1) Out of 180 GNVQ students, 35% gained a pass, 40% a merit and 25% a distinction.
   a) Show this data in a bar chart. b) Change the bar chart into a pie chart.

Frequency Distributions

A frequency distribution can be as simple as a bar chart. You might get distributions like these from doing a survey questionnaire or a probability experiment. See Section 3 for Mean, Median and Mode.

Frequency Distributions have Different Shapes

Here are five examples showing possible shapes of frequency distributions. You need to be able to describe the shape of a distribution. Notice that the frequency density always goes up the y-axis.

1 Symmetrical Distribution
Mode = Median = Mean

f. d.

Modal Class — the class (along the x-axis) that has the highest frequency.

2 Bimodal Distribution

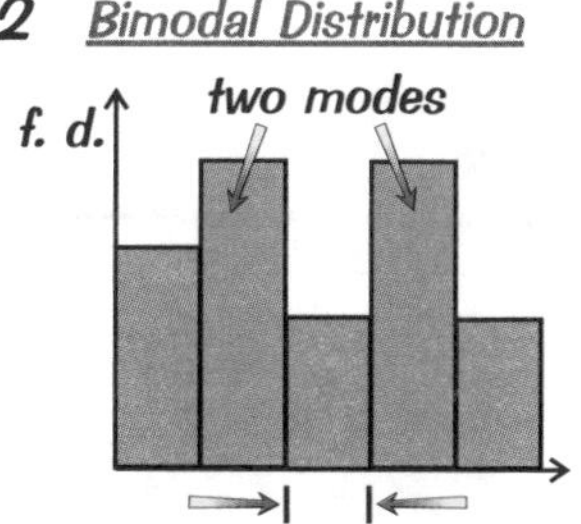

The class width is how wide a bar is.

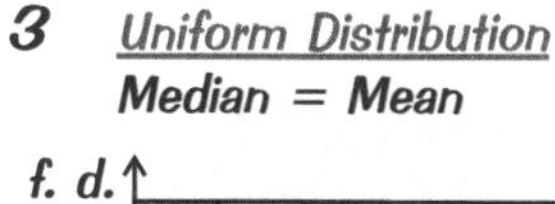

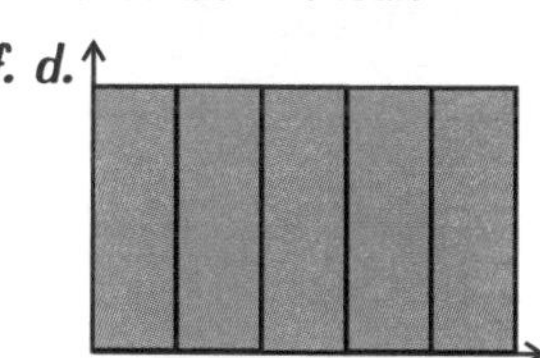

A uniform distribution doesn't have a modal class.

4 Positive Skew
Mode < Median < Mean

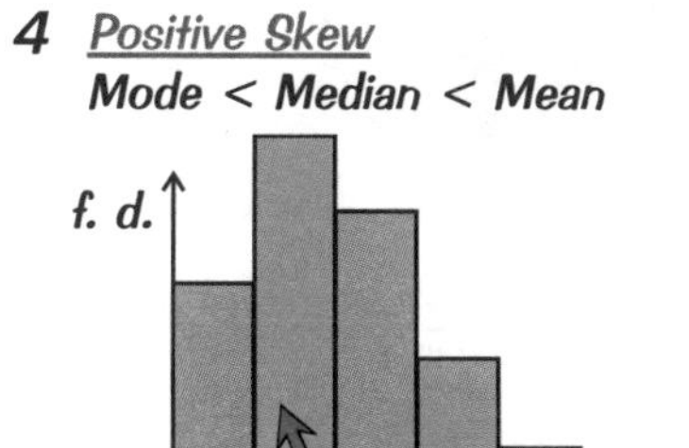

The data is bunched to the left

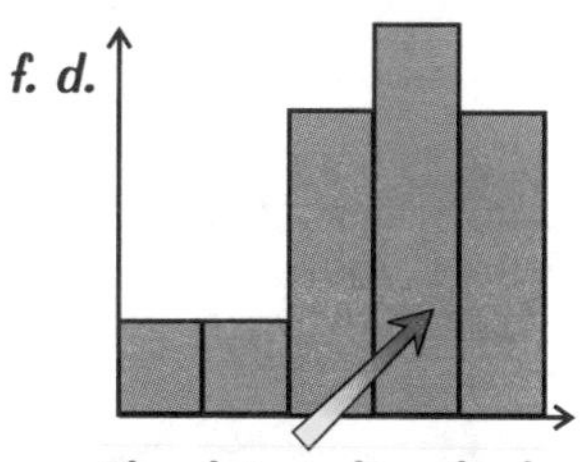

The data is bunched to the right

A Normal Distribution is Drawn as a Smooth Curve

Take the symmetrical example above. If you make the class widths smaller and smaller, so you've got more and more bars, you eventually get a smooth curve. This is called the Normal Distribution.

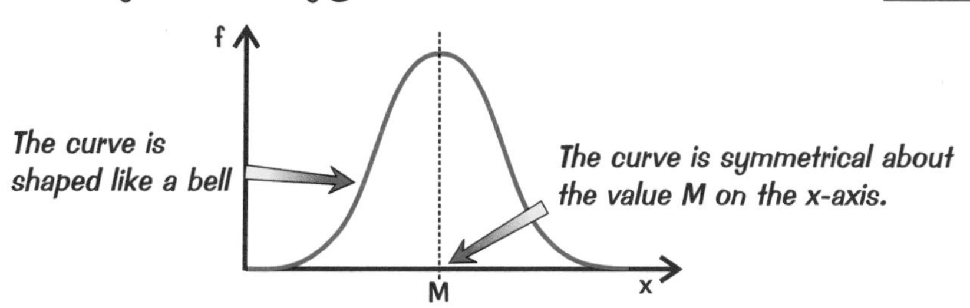

The mean, median and mode are all the same and equal to M.
The distribution is symmetrical around M.

Higher

The Acid Test:

Before you move on from this page, make sure you can recognise ALL the different distributions on this page.

1) Sketch a histogram of a frequency distribution that has six equal class widths and positive skew.

2) The graph shows the number of children of different ages attending a playgroup.
   a) What is the modal group?
   b) Describe the shape of the distribution.
   c) What is the total number of children in the group?

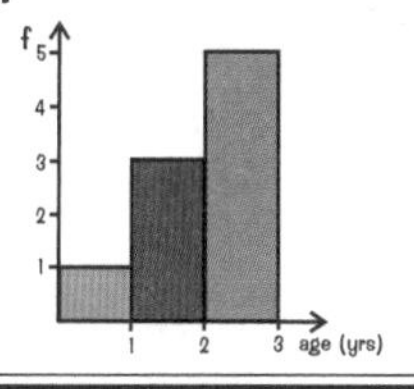

Scatter Diagrams and Time Series

Scatter diagrams show two variables on the same graph.
A scatter diagram tells you if the two things are related.

Draw a Line of Best Fit if there is a Relationship

If there is a relationship between the two variables then you can draw a line of best fit through the points on the graph.

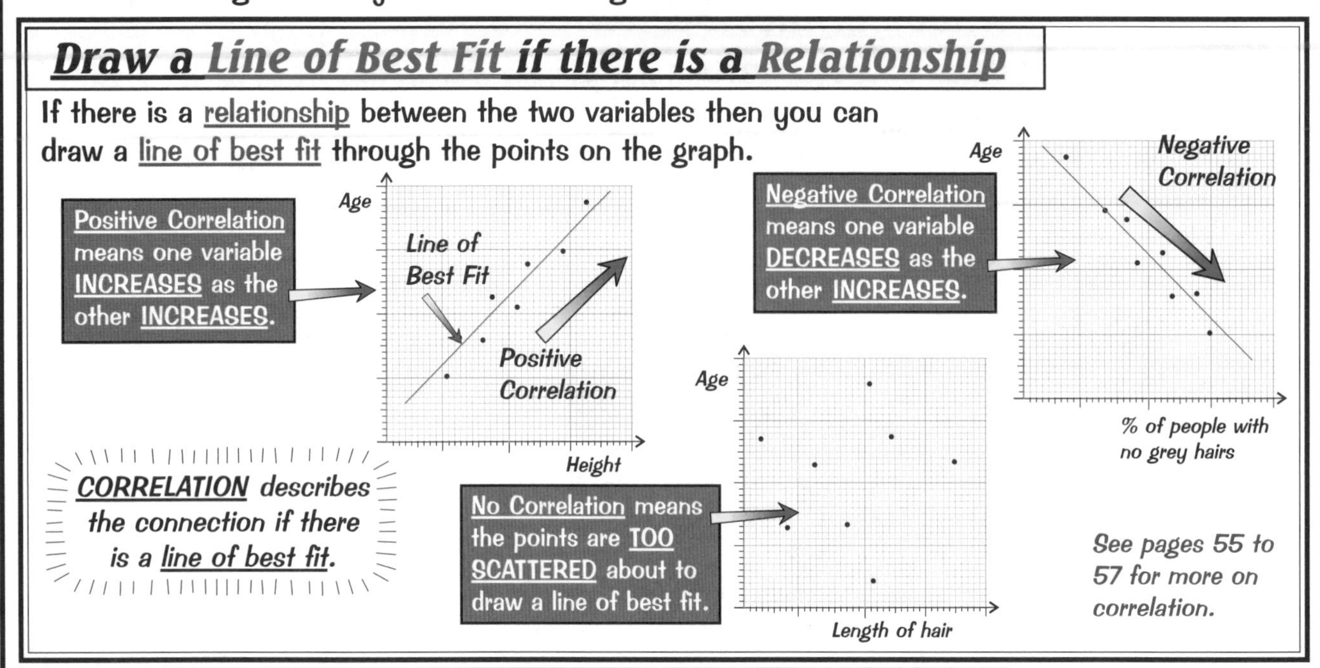

See pages 55 to 57 for more on correlation.

Time Series are plotted with Time on the x-Axis

A time series is a set of data values obtained at successive times.
They are plotted with TIME on the x-axis — and you join the points together.

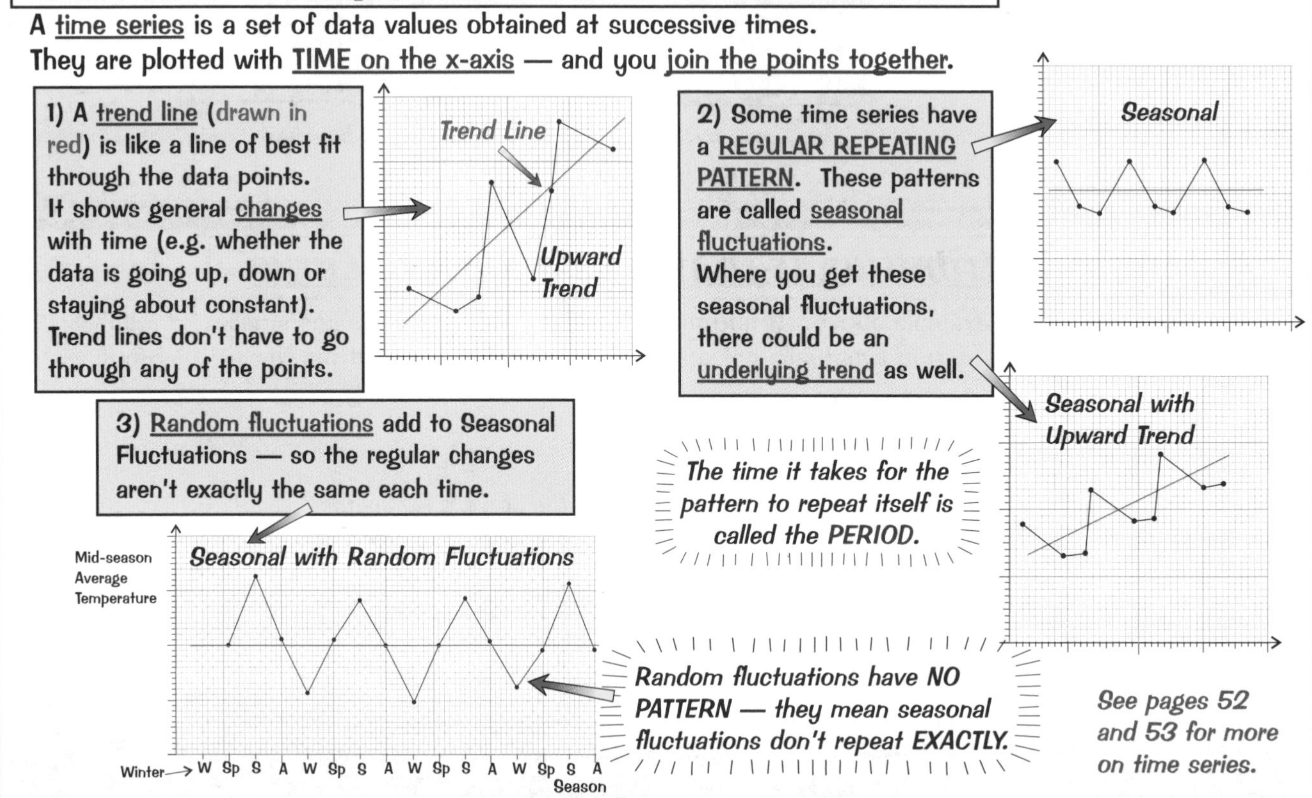

See pages 52 and 53 for more on time series.

The Acid Test:

Learn the definitions of CORRELATION, TIME SERIES, TREND LINES, SEASONAL FLUCTUATIONS and PERIOD.

1) My town's rainfall is measured every month for 20 years and the rainfall in mm is plotted against the time in months. There is a rough pattern which repeats itself every 12 months, and the amount of rain each month is decreasing each year relative to the year before.
a) How would you describe this data? b) What is the period?

More Diagrams, Problems and Errors

There are lots of different ways to represent data. Some of them can be a bit misleading...

Pictograms can Sometimes be Confusing

In this pictogram, pictures of bags show how high the bars are. The bags are cut to size. This is a good way of showing accurate heights.

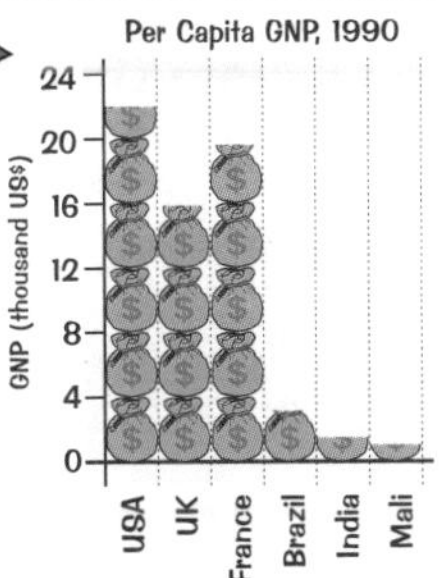

In this pictogram some bags have been squashed.

The heights of the bars are correct, BUT you might think the squashed bags are worth the same as an 'unsquashed' bag because they're still complete bags.

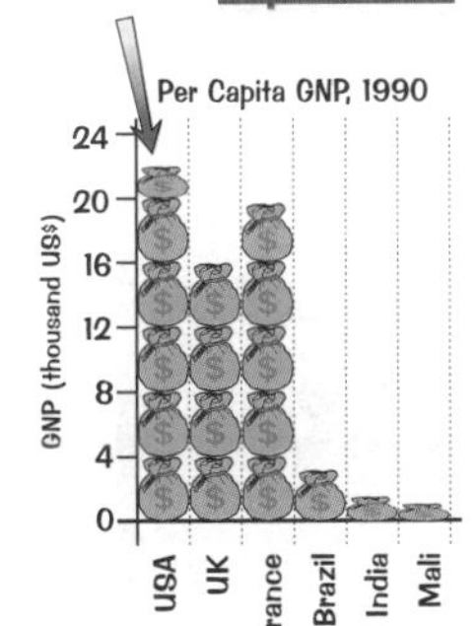

Pie Charts can be Used and Abused

This pie chart has four equal sectors. The angles for A, B, C and D are equal.

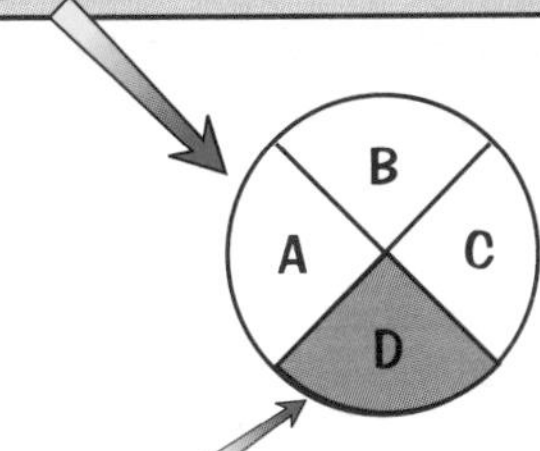

Using brighter colours for some parts of a chart makes them stand out more.

The same pie chart is then made to look three-dimensional. Sectors B and D now cover more of the page than A and C. They appear bigger to the eye even though all four are the same. This can be misleading.

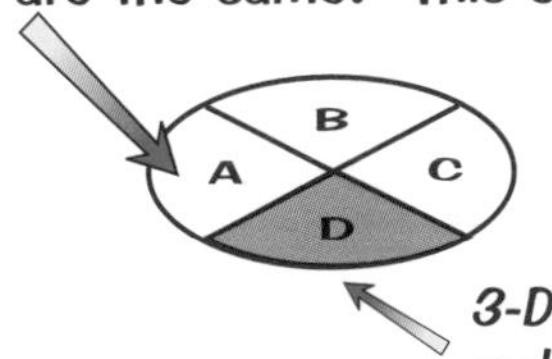

3-D View — sectors B and D look BIGGER

Volume should be treated with Care

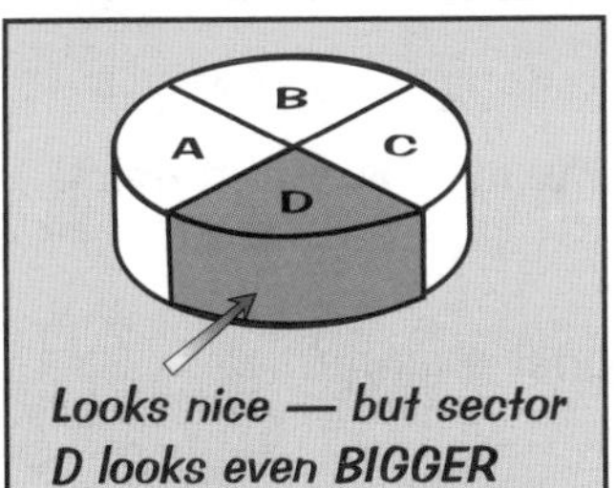

The same pie chart now has volume.
Sector D covers more of the page than any of the other three.
The pie chart is still accurate, but sector D looks more important than the others. You often see this sort of thing in reports and the press.

In the bar charts below, bars A and C are equal in height.

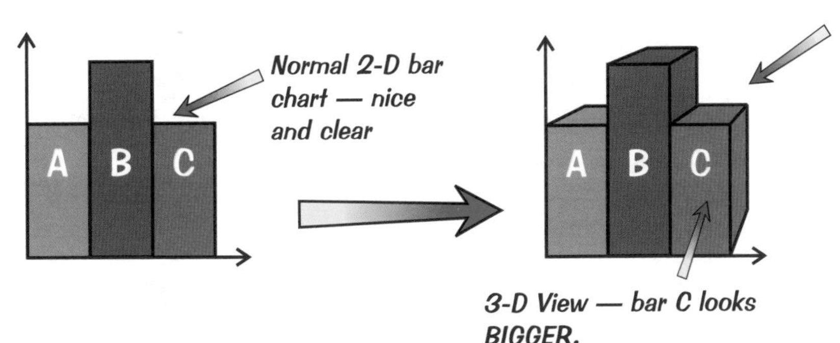

The same bar chart now has VOLUME. Bar C now appears to be bigger.
It covers about the same area of the page as bar B.
Bar A might seem less important as it is partly hidden behind bar B.

You need to think when using three dimensions. There's nothing actually WRONG with these diagrams, but you need to read them more carefully because they can be a bit misleading.

More Diagrams, Problems and Errors

Making your diagrams look nice isn't always a good idea — you can really confuse people...

Watch out for Scale Factors, Area Factors and Volume Factors

Remember that if all the LENGTHs are DOUBLED on a diagram, the AREA of the diagram becomes FOUR TIMES as big (2^2) and the VOLUME becomes EIGHT TIMES as big (2^3).

A sports shop sold twice as many footballs in 2003 as it did in 2002.
The three diagrams below try to show this data — but only the first one is clear:

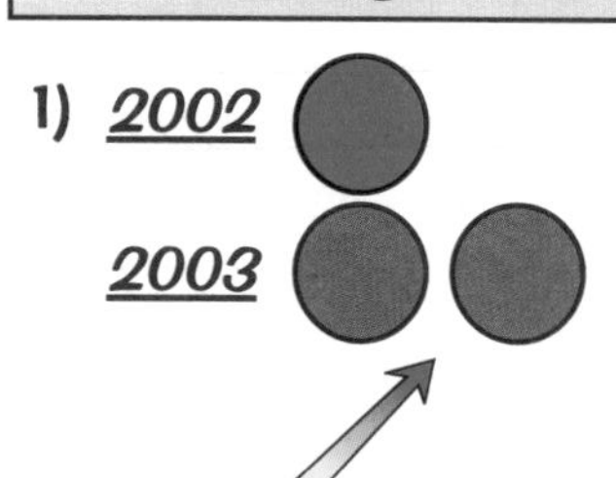

This first diagram is clear and not misleading. The area for 2003 is twice that for 2002.

2) 2002

four times the area

2003

The diameter of the 2003 disc is double that of the 2002 disc. This means it has FOUR TIMES the area (Scale Factor squared), which is misleading. If the area had been doubled it would be OK.

3) 2002

eight times the volume

2003

This three-dimensional 2003 'football' has a volume of eight times the 2002 'football' (Scale Factor cubed). Again this could be very confusing.

If you want to use Area and Volume — Do it Properly

If you decide you do want to use area or volume — here's how to do it right.

EXAMPLE: The salary bonus for a company employee trebles from one year to the next. The company manager wants to show this in a diagram. She decides to do it in three ways — as a linear increase, an area increase and a volume increase.

Method 1: Linear Increase — starting with a 10 mm long bar

This is like a bar in a chart. Its LENGTH becomes three times what it was. Nice and easy...

10 mm 30 mm

The thickness of the bar / line does not increase. It's a one-dimensional change.

Method 2: Area Increase — starting with a 10 mm square

The AREA must be three times what it was — i.e. $3 \times 100\text{ mm}^2 = 300\text{ mm}^2$

10 mm

The new square has sides of x mm.

$x \times x = 300$ $x = \sqrt{300}$ $x = 17\text{ mm}$ (2 S.F.)

Simply multiplying the sides of the square by three would be wrong, and would make the bonus look nine times the original value...

Method 3: Volume Increase — starting with a 10 mm cube

Here the new VOLUME must be three times what it was — i.e. $3 \times 1000\text{ mm}^3 = 3000\text{ mm}^3$

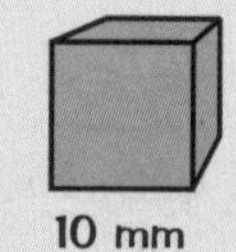

The new cube has sides of $\sqrt[3]{3000} = 14\text{ mm}$ (2 S.F.)

More Diagrams, Problems and Errors

More things can go wrong with graphs than you can shake a badger at*...

Graphs can lead you up the Garden Path...

Graph A below shows some information accurately — the others are more confusing or misleading.

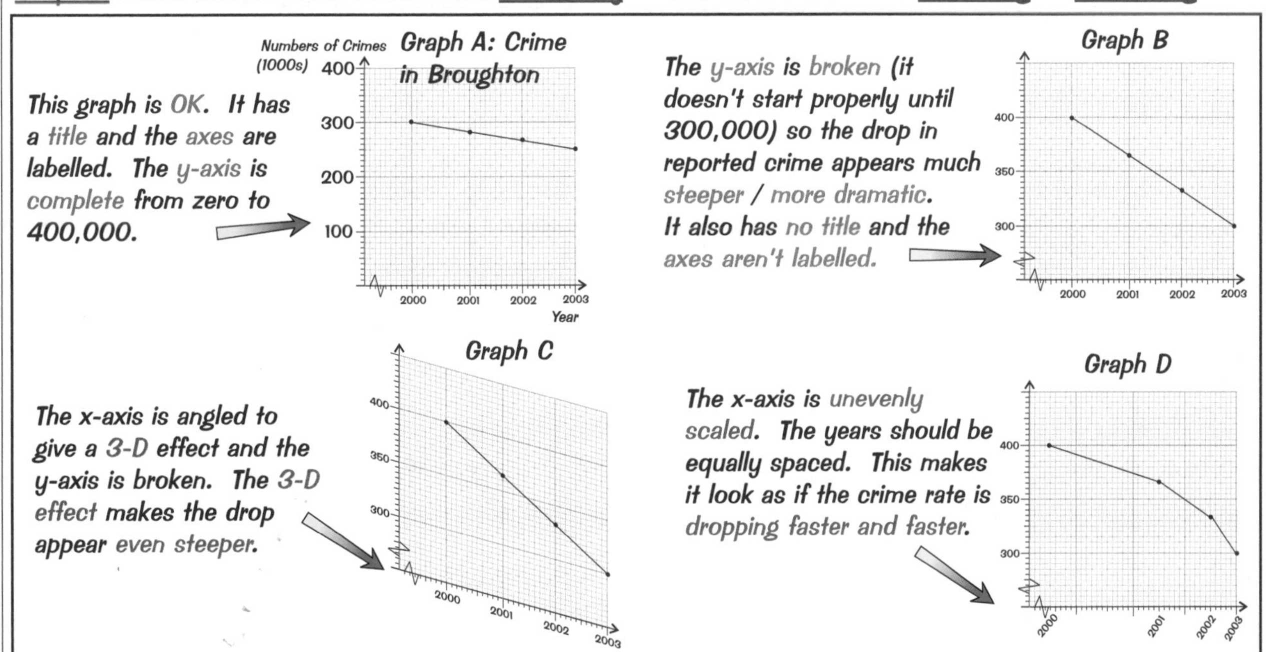

Make sure your graph has labelled axes, with correct units, and a title explaining what the graph shows. Try NOT to break the y-axis and check the numbers on the axes aren't misleading. Be careful that colour and 3-D effects don't make the graph confusing.

Outliers don't fit the General Pattern

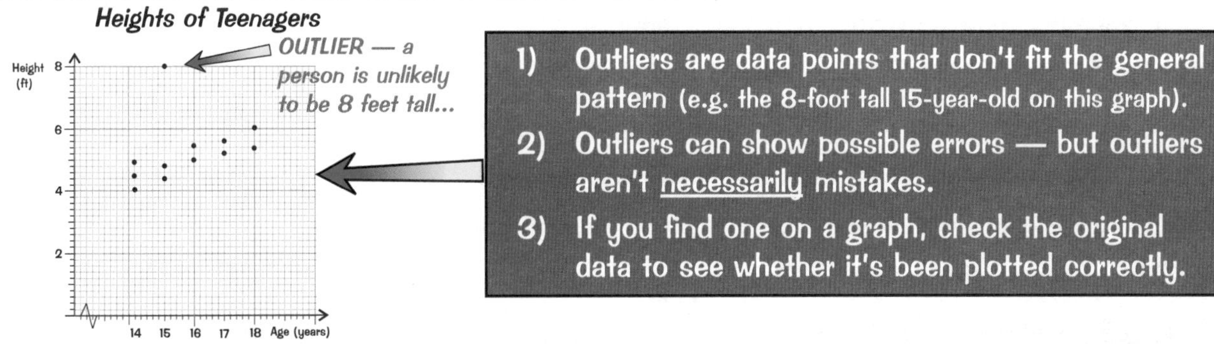

1) Outliers are data points that don't fit the general pattern (e.g. the 8-foot tall 15-year-old on this graph).
2) Outliers can show possible errors — but outliers aren't necessarily mistakes.
3) If you find one on a graph, check the original data to see whether it's been plotted correctly.

The Acid Test:

Learn everything from these three pages. Be aware of all the ways in which diagrams can mislead people.

1) Each of these three diagrams is misleading in at least one way. How? Explain fully.

2) This diagram has several problems. What are they? Explain fully.

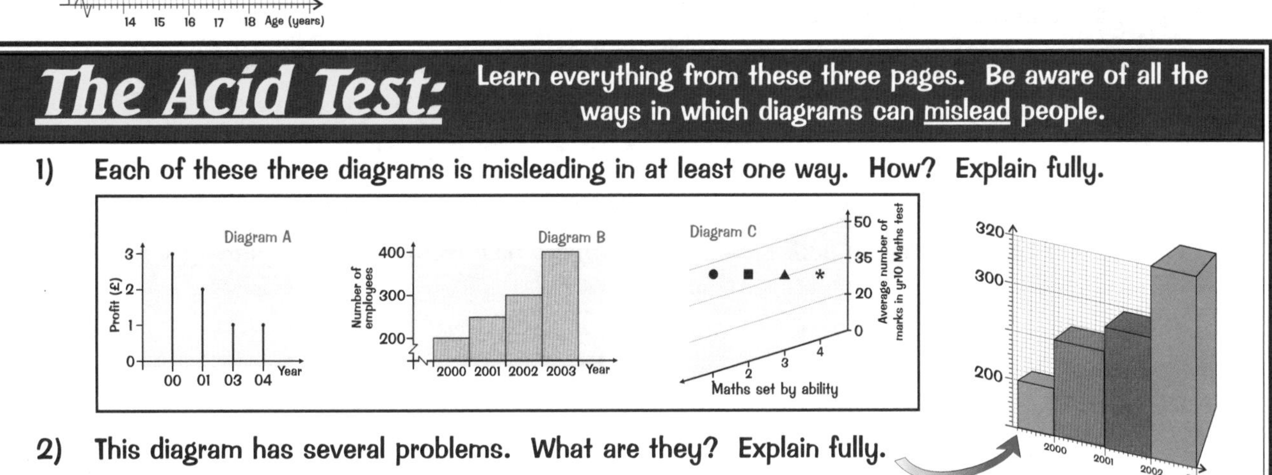

* Pleas note: CGP does not advocate the shaking of badgers.

Revision Summary for Section Two

Here's what you've really been waiting for — a nice page of questions to get your teeth into. Doing these questions will give you the clearest idea of where you need to do more revision. If you struggle with any, go back and go over that part of the section again...

Keep learning the basic facts until you know them

1) Why is it important to keep a tally when doing a frequency table?
2) When and why do you use grouped frequency tables?
3) Describe the advantages and disadvantages of simplifying a table by totalling.
4) Why might you convert the data in a table into percentages?
5) How can reducing the number of classes in a grouped frequency table make the table misleading?
6) How is data represented in pictograms?
7) Describe two types of graph for representing discrete data.
8) How do graphs of discrete data differ from graphs of continuous data?
9) Describe how to plot a frequency polygon.
10) Describe how to change a frequency polygon into a cumulative frequency polygon.
11) How is a population pyramid useful for making comparisons?
12) Is a histogram the same as a bar chart? If not, describe how they are different.
13) What is frequency density in a histogram? How do you calculate frequency density?
14) How do you find the frequency represented by a bar in a histogram?
15) What is the 'stem' and what is the 'leaf' in a stem and leaf diagram?
16) Describe one advantage of using a stem and leaf diagram.
17) How is information represented on a choropleth map?
18) How might a choropleth map be useful in geography?
19) Describe the process for changing a bar chart into a pie chart.
20) What's the method for changing a pie chart into a bar chart?
21) Sketch a bar chart to show a frequency distribution with positive skew.
22) Sketch a normal distribution.
23) What is the purpose of a scatter graph?
24) Describe what it means for two variables to be negatively correlated.
25) On a time series graph:
    a) What does a trend line show? b) What are seasonal fluctuations?
26) Why should you be careful when using 3-D, volume and colour in diagrams? Give examples.
27) What is an outlier? Does an outlier always mean there has been an error in plotting a graph?

Mean, Median and Mode

Once you've collected your data, you need to make sense of what you've got — you need the 3 M's.

The Arithmetic Mean is the "Average"

The "arithmetic mean" is usually just called the "mean".

ADD TOGETHER all the data values and DIVIDE by the total number of values in the sample.

EXAMPLE: Number of people living in each of nine three-bedroomed houses:

3 5 1 3 7 5 5 5 2

Mean = (3 + 5 + 1 + 3 + 7 + 5 + 5 + 5 + 2)/9 = 4

The mean changes if you add or remove a data value from the sample (unless it's equal to the mean itself).
If you add a value greater than the mean or take away a value less than the mean — the mean increases.
If you add a value less than the mean or take away a value greater — it decreases.

Higher

Finding the Mean for Large Numbers

AQA only

A neat little trick — take a number away from all the values (so you only have to deal with small numbers) and find the mean of those. Then add the number you took away back onto the result.

For example, to find the mean of the following numbers, take away 190 first.

191 192 199 198 196 194 195

Mean = 190 + (1 + 2 + 9 + 8 + 6 + 4 + 5)/7 = 190 + 5 = 195

A weighted meanie

The Weighted Mean

Edexcel only

This is used to combine different sets of data when one is more important than another.

EXAMPLE: If 25% of your GCSE is coursework then this carries a weight of 0.25, and the exam marks will carry a weight of 0.75.
So, if you score 70% for coursework and 55% for your exam then your percentage result will be (70 × 0.25) + (55 × 0.75) = 58.75%

The Median is the Middle Value

First put the data in ascending order, then find the middle value.
It's easy to find if you've got an odd number of values.
If there's an even number of values, the median is halfway between the two middle values.

For example, with data values: 5 8 ↑ 10 12,

the median comes halfway between the 8 and the 10 so Median = 9

If there are n data values, the position of the median is (n + 1)/2.

The Mode is the One that Appears Most Often

You can find the mode either by inspection (just looking at the data) or using a tally chart.
So in the data set: 3, 5, 1, 3, 7, 5, 5, 5, 2, the Mode is 5 (it appears 4 times)

The Acid Test:

Make sure you know what the three M's are and how to find them for any given set of data.

1) These are marks obtained by a school's top ten maths students: 98, 99, 97, 91, 97, 92, 93, 97, 95, 98
Find: a) the mean b) the median c) the mode
2) A music exam allocates 40% of the practical marks and 60% of the theory marks to the final result.
If a student scores 60% in the practical and 80% in the theory, what is their overall percentage?

Mean, Median and Mode

It can make sense to record your data in a table — you get what's called a frequency distribution.

Discrete Frequency Distributions are for Countable Data

Countable things like shoe sizes or the number of fish in a pond are discrete data (see p.2).

EXAMPLE: Number of sweets in each of one hundred packets sampled:

Number of sweets	38	39	40	41	42	43
Number of packets	5	18	29	33	13	2

Understanding the Table

A table like this is just a set of RAW DATA put into a different format.

1) The sample data means that there are 5 packets of 38 sweets, 18 packets of 39 sweets, etc.
2) You find the MEAN in exactly the same way as you did before. Add all the values together (remember that $38 + 38 + 38 + 38 + 38 = 5 \times 38$, etc.) and divide by the total number of values.
   Mean $= [(5 \times 38)+(18 \times 39)+(29 \times 40)+(33 \times 41)+(13 \times 42)+(2 \times 43)]/100 = 40.37$
3) The MEDIAN is still the middle value but you have to count down through the table to find it. One advantage of the table is that the data's already in ascending order.
   Median position $= (n + 1)/2 = (100 + 1)/2 = 50.5$ (see p.41)
   This means that the median value lies between the 50th and the 51st packets.
   Looking at the table, there are $5 + 18 = 23$ values in the first two columns.
   And $23 + 29 = 52$ in the first three. So, the 50th and 51st values must be in the third column, and the median must be 40.
4) The MODE is easy to find from grouped data as the frequencies have already been worked out. The mode is 41 as more packets hold 41 sweets than any other number.

Continuous data tends to be recorded in GROUPS

Continuous data is often recorded in a grouped frequency table, using inequalities (see p.25).

EXAMPLE:

Length (mm)	$85 < x \leq 90$	$90 < x \leq 95$	$95 < x \leq 100$	$100 < x \leq 105$	$105 < x \leq 110$
Frequency	3	7	15	10	5
Midpoint (mm)	87.5	92.5	97.5	102.5	107.5

Since you don't know the individual data values, you can only ESTIMATE the mean.
You estimate the mean using the midpoint values from each group,
e.g. the midpoint of the first group is $(85+90)/2 = 87.5$.

So Mean $= [(3 \times 87.5)+(7 \times 92.5)+(15 \times 97.5)+(10 \times 102.5)+(5 \times 107.5)]/40 = 98.375$ mm

The Modal group is the group with the most entries, which is $95 < x \leq 100$.

The Median is the value in position number $(40 + 1)/2$, which is also in the group $95 < x \leq 100$.

The Acid Test:

Learn everything on this page, making sure you understand the different ways the data has been represented.

1)

Number of questions	15	16	17	18	19	20	21
Number of Exam Papers	3	6	7	12	9	5	2

a) Calculate the mean number of questions per paper. b) Find the median. c) What is the mode?

2)

Weight (g)	$3 < x \leq 6$	$6 < x \leq 9$	$9 < x \leq 12$	$12 < x \leq 15$
Frequency	1	9	5	3
Midpoint				

a) Complete the table and calculate the mean.
b) In which group is the median?
c) What is the modal group?

Mean, Median and Mode

The mean, median and mode all have their advantages and disadvantages:

	Advantages	Disadvantages
Mean	Uses all the data Usually most representative	Is not always a data value May be distorted by outliers
Median	Easy to find in ordered data Not distorted by outliers	Is not always a data value Not always a good representation of the data
Mode	Easy to find in tallied data Always a data value	Doesn't always exist Sometimes more than one

Choose the Most Appropriate Average

THE MEAN:
1) It tends to be the most useful, since it uses all the data in its calculation.
2) Outliers affect its accuracy, but they can be got round by choosing a larger sample.
3) The mean's often used to compare performances of people or items, such as cricketers' batting averages, golfers' handicaps or the lifetimes of batteries.

THE MEDIAN:
1) It only gives you the middle value, but becomes more useful when used together with the range and interquartile range (see p.44 and 45).

THE MODE:
1) It's an easy way of telling you which data value is most likely to appear.
2) It's mainly used with discrete data, as continuous data might not have two values the same.
3) It can give a misleading value. Look at this data giving you the weight in grams of each of ten eggs:
   59 65 66 64 63 69 68 69 61 62
   The mode is 69 g — which is a long way from the mean weight, 64.6 g.
4) One advantage the mode has over the mean and median is that it can be used in qualitative data.
   E.g. Which school subject is the most popular? What flavour ice cream sells the most?

There's a Geometric Mean as well as the Arithmetic Mean

You can use the geometric mean to combine two or more interest rates into one.
The geometric mean of n numbers is:

$$\text{Geometric Mean} = \sqrt[n]{x_1 \times x_2 \times \ldots \times x_n}$$

EXAMPLE: *An investment receives 3% interest in the 1st year, 4% in the 2nd and 8% in the 3rd. What annual rate of interest would give the same return over the three years?*

To find the value of the investment after three years, multiply it by $1.03 \times 1.04 \times 1.08$

Geometric Mean = $\sqrt[3]{1.03 \times 1.04 \times 1.08} = 1.04978$

So, Annual Interest = 4.978%

The Acid Test:

When you think you have mastered the three M's and can find the geometric mean, answer the following questions.

1) State which average would be the most suitable for each of these sets of data:
   a) 22, 26, 31, 24, 23, 27, 46, 22
   b) Red, Blue, Red, Green, Blue, Red, Green, Red
   c) 3, 3, 3, 3, 4, 8, 9, 9
2) Find the geometric mean of 4, 7 and 9.

Higher

Range and Quartiles

Finding the range is about as easy as it gets. Quartiles are just that little bit harder — but more useful.

The Range — How far the Data Spreads

To find the RANGE of a set of data you just work out the DIFFERENCE between the HIGHEST and the LOWEST number.

EXAMPLE: Find the range of these numbers: 7, 12, 5, 4, 3, 7, 5, 11, 6, 4, 9

ANSWER: Highest number – Lowest number = 12 – 3

The range is 9. It's a really simple way of giving you an idea of the spread of data.

Finding the Quartiles is bit more tricky

QUARTILES divide the data into four equal groups. They're known as the LOWER QUARTILE Q_1, the MEDIAN Q_2 and the UPPER QUARTILE Q_3. If you put the data in ascending order, the quartiles are 25% (¼), 50% (½) and 75% (¾) of the way through the list.

If you get non-integer values for $(n + 1)/4$ or $3(n + 1)/4$, round UP. If you get a non-integer value for $(n + 1)/2$, use the two values EITHER SIDE.

METHOD:

1) Put the data in ASCENDING ORDER.
2) Work out where the QUARTILES come in the list using the following formulas:
   - Q_1 position number = $(n + 1)/4$
   - Q_2 position number = $2(n + 1)/4$
   - Q_3 position number = $3(n + 1)/4$

E.g. using the same set of data as before,

7 12 5 4 3 7 5 11 6 4 9

Step 1: n = 11 so Q_1 position no. = $(11 + 1)/4 = 3$

Q_2 position no. = $2(11 + 1)/4 = 6$

Q_3 position no. = $3(11 + 1)/4 = 9$

Step 2: 3 4 4 5 5 6 7 7 9 11 12

Q_1 (position 3), Q_2 (position 6), Q_3 (position 9); position 1 ... position 11

3) So, the lower quartile Q_1 = 4, the median Q_2 = 6 and the upper quartile Q_3 = 9.

You can use more groups to give you a more flexible view of the spread of data.

DECILES, D_1 to D_9 divide the data into ten equal groups.

PERCENTILES, P_1 to P_{99}, divide the data into one hundred equal groups.

$Q_2 = D_5 = P_{50}$, all of which represent the median.

The formulas to work out the positions of deciles and percentiles are really similar to the ones for working out quartiles: D_1 position no. = $(n + 1)/10$, D_2 position no. = $2(n + 1)/10$, ...

P_1 position no. = $(n + 1)/100$, P_2 position no. = $2(n + 1)/100$, ...

The Acid Test:

Learn how to find the range, quartiles, deciles and percentiles and then answer these questions.

1) What does the 'range' mean?
2) For the list of integers from 1 to 999 inclusive:
   a) What is the range?
   b) What is the value of the upper quartile?
   c) Find D_2, the 2nd decile.
   d) Calculate the 85th percentile.

Interquartile and Interpercentile Range

Interquartile means "Between Quartiles"

The INTERQUARTILE RANGE is the difference between the upper quartile and the lower quartile.

EXAMPLE: Find the interquartile range of the data from p44:

3 4 4 5 5 6 7 7 9 11 12

ANSWER: Upper quartile = 9 Lower quartile = 4 Interquartile range = 9 – 4 = 5

Exam questions usually give you a grouped frequency table and ask you to plot a cumulative frequency curve from it. Then you just follow the steps to find the interquartile or percentile range.

EXAMPLE: Find the interquartile range and the $P_{90} - P_{10}$ percentile range of the following data.

Time taken for each of 200 people to solve a puzzle:

time (mins)	frequency	cumulative frequency
$0 \le t < 5$	8	8
$5 \le t < 10$	30	38
$10 \le t < 15$	66	104
$15 \le t < 20$	58	162
$20 \le t < 25$	26	188
$25 \le t < 30$	12	200

If you don't understand this table — better check out 'Cumulative Frequency' again (see p.30).

Step 1: PLOT and draw the CUMULATIVE FREQUENCY CURVE.

Step 2: Draw horizontal lines from the 25% and 75% marks on the y-axis to the cumulative frequency curve and read off the corresponding x-values. These are Q_1 and Q_3 respectively.

Step 3: Calculate the DIFFERENCE between Q_1 and Q_3 to give the INTERQUARTILE RANGE i.e. $Q_3 - Q_1 = 18.5 - 11 = 7.5$

Step 4: Draw horizontal lines from the 10% and 90% marks on the y-axis to the cumulative frequency curve and read off the corresponding x-values. These are P_{10} and P_{90} respectively.

Step 5: Calculate the difference to give the P_{90} TO P_{10} PERCENTILE RANGE i.e. $P_{90} - P_{10} = 23 - 7.5 = 15.5$

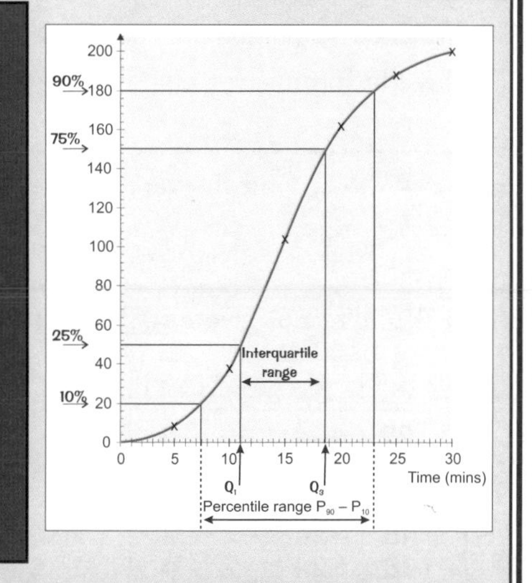

1) The interquartile range tells you the range of the middle 50% of the data — where most of the activity's going on — so it's often more useful than the range itself.

Higher

2) Small percentile ranges let you see what's going on in smaller areas of the data. This is most useful when the data's irregular, or isn't symmetrical about the mean (skewed).

3) The P_{90} to P_{10} percentile range gives a more realistic idea of the spread of data than the range does. It gives the range of the middle 80% of the data, ignoring any outliers.

Higher

The Acid Test:

Learn how to find the interquartile range and the percentiles and then cover up the page and answer these questions.

1) Write down the odd numbers between 1 and 13 inclusive. What is the interquartile range?

2) Look at the cumulative frequency curve on the right. Find:

a) the interquartile range,

b) the P_{20} and P_{80} percentiles, and hence

c) the $P_{80} - P_{20}$ percentile range.

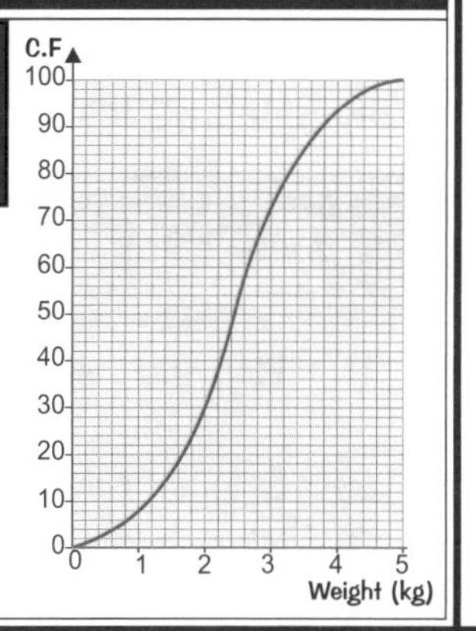

Variance and Standard Deviation

These two use all the data — harder to find but much more useful than ranges.

Variance — How Much the Data Varies from the Mean

The variance (σ^2) of a set of data values is the mean of the squared deviations from their mean.

Eeeeek!! OK, it sounds scary — but all you really have to do is learn how to use some formulas and sharpen up your calculator skills.

$\sum$, the Greek letter sigma, just means "the sum of".

For a set of n data values $x_1, x_2, \ldots, x_n$ whose mean is $\bar{x}$,

$\sum(x-\bar{x})^2$ is the sum of "the squared deviations from their mean".

So, the formula for finding the variance is $\frac{\sum(x-\bar{x})^2}{n}$

An alternative formula that's easier to use is $\frac{\sum x^2}{n} - \bar{x}^2$

You don't need to learn these formulas — you'll be given them in the exam. You do need to KNOW WHAT THEY MEAN though.

Standard Deviation is Easy once you've found the Variance

Variance = (Standard deviation)^2

So, the formula for standard deviation (σ) is: $\sigma = \sqrt{\frac{\sum(x-\bar{x})^2}{n}}$ or $\sigma = \sqrt{\frac{\sum x^2}{n} - \bar{x}^2}$

EXAMPLE: Find the variance and standard deviation of the following data:

22 20 25 18 18 18 19 20

n = 8, mean $\bar{x}$ = 160/8 = 20

If you're not given a table to complete then MAKE YOUR OWN.

x	x^2	$(x-\bar{x})$	$(x-\bar{x})^2$
22	484	2	4
20	400	0	0
25	625	5	25
18	324	–2	4
18	324	–2	4
18	324	–2	4
19	361	–1	1
20	400	0	0
160	3242		42

$\sum x^2$ (3242), $\sum(x-\bar{x})^2$ (42)

1) List the data values in the first column.
2) What you put in the other columns depends on which set of formulas you're using. I've colour-coded the columns in my table — you only need to use the ones that match the set of formulas you're using.
3) So, using the "purple" formulas:

$\sigma^2 = 42/8 = 5.25$ and $\sigma = \sqrt{5.25} = 2.29$

Using the "yellow" formulas:

$\sigma^2 = (3242/8) - 20^2 = 5.25$ and $\sigma = \sqrt{5.25} = 2.29$

Variance = 5.25 and Standard Deviation = 2.29

Variance and Standard Deviation are Measures of Spread

Both the variance and standard deviation tell you how spread out the data is.
The SMALLER they are, the closer the data is to the mean.

The Acid Test:

Make sure you understand all the symbols used.

1) Find the variance and standard deviation of the following numbers:
   –1 4 –2 5 3 2 2 1 0 1
2) Calculate the standard deviation of the first six odd numbers.
3) What is the standard deviation of the first six even numbers?

Box and Whisker Plots

A box and whisker plot is pretty much what it says it is — a box with whiskers, one on either side.

Box and Whisker Plots Show the Interquartile Range

The total length of a box and whisker plot (or box plot as it's more commonly known) represents the range of the data. The middle 50% of the data is the box and the rest is the whiskers.

1) Draw a LINE to scale to represent the range.
2) Mark the upper and lower quartiles and draw the BOX.
3) Finally, draw a LINE DOWN THE BOX at the median.

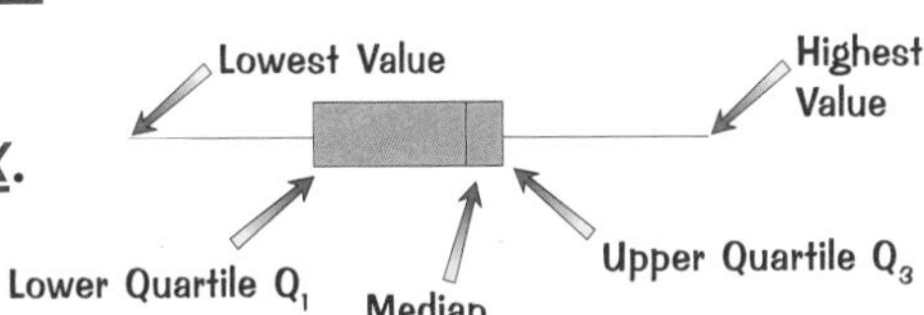

EXAMPLE: Draw a box plot with a minimum of 0, a range of 18, a median equal to 13 and upper and lower quartiles equal to 14 and 8 respectively.

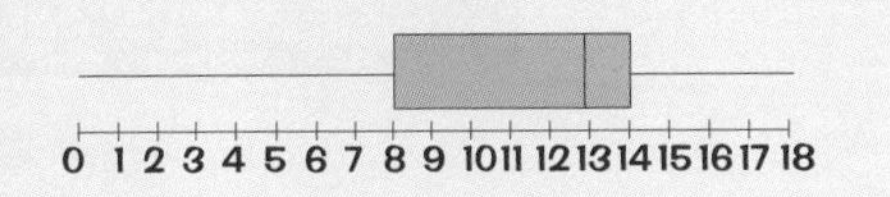

With the data in the form of a box plot you can get a good idea of the spread of the data on sight.

It's fairly easy to draw a box plot under a CUMULATIVE FREQUENCY GRAPH.

1) You can extend the vertical lines used to read off the values of the quartiles to form the box.
2) The start and end of the graph mark the ends of the whiskers.

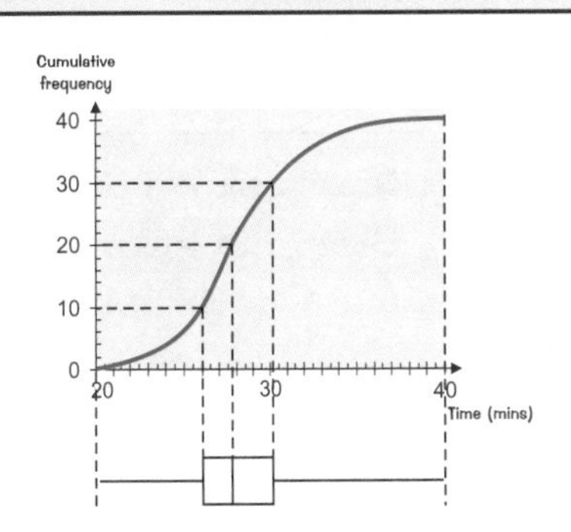

Outliers are Values a Long Way from the Mean

Higher

OUTLIERS are values that are out on their own, a long way from the mean. These little monsters can distort an otherwise reasonable set of data — so you need to identify them.
The usual way to identify outliers is to look for any values that are more than one and a half times the interquartile range away from the upper or lower quartiles.

Outliers are values $> Q_3 + 1.5(Q_3 - Q_1)$ or values $< Q_1 - 1.5(Q_3 - Q_1)$

Skip the rest of this if you're doing Edexcel.

A BOX PLOT helps you find the outliers because the range of the data and the upper and lower quartiles are there for you to see.

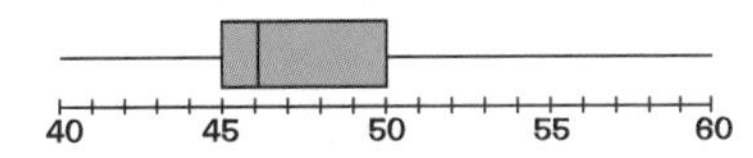

$Q_3 + 1.5(Q_3 - Q_1) = 50 + 1.5(50 - 45) = \underline{57.5}$
$Q_1 - 1.5(Q_3 - Q_1) = 45 - 1.5(50 - 45) = \underline{37.5}$

Mark outliers with a cross.

This means you can identify the outliers as any data values that are greater than 57.5 or less than 37.5. If there are any outliers, the whiskers should be shortened to extend to the highest and lowest data values that are not outliers.

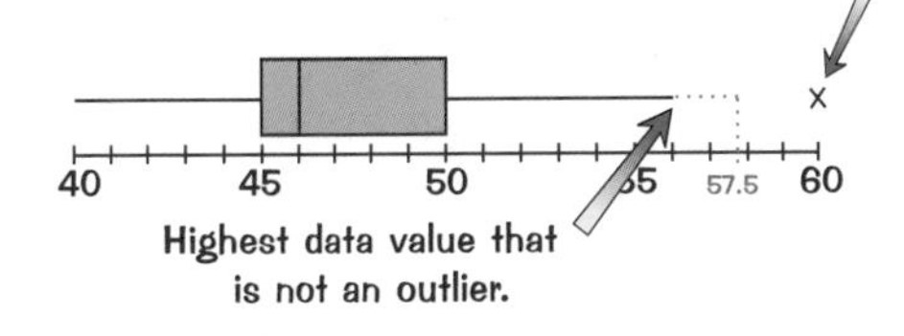

The Acid Test:

Learn everything on this page and make sure you remember how to find the median and the interquartile range.

1) These are the times in minutes that eleven birthday cake candles stayed alight:
13 15 12 16 2 14 14 9 13 13 17
a) Draw a box plot to represent this data.
b) Identify any outliers and redraw the box plot.

Standardised Scores

Standardised scores are used to compare values from different sets of data.

Formula for Finding the Standardised Score

You can't compare individual values from two different data sets DIRECTLY, e.g. you couldn't compare an exam mark from something easy like Media Studies with a mark from a proper subject like Physics (stir, stir). You need to STANDARDISE them first.

$$\text{standardised score} = \frac{\text{value} - \text{mean}}{\text{standard deviation}}$$

Standardised scorers

Any value equal to the mean has a standardised score of ZERO (you can see that from the formula) — so zero is an average score.

Anything ABOVE ZERO is better than average and anything NEGATIVE is below average.

EXAMPLE: Nick took his GCSE Maths and English along with the rest of his year. Given the following information, work out his standardised scores and state in which subject he did the best.

Subject	Score	Mean	Standard Deviation
Maths	60%	70%	1.8
English	65%	72%	1.2

Standardised score for Maths = (60 – 70)/1.8 = –5.6

Standardised score for English = (65 – 72)/1.2 = –5.8

This means that Nick's best performance was in the Maths exam, since his standardised score was higher in that than in English.

Both the scores in this example are out of 100 (i.e. a percentage), but they don't have to be. You can compare a score out of 50 with one out of, say, 7842 — it makes no difference.

This formula only strictly applies if both sets of data follow a Normal Distribution (p.35). You don't really need to worry about that though.

The Acid Test:

Learn the formula — it is one of the easiest ones to remember.

1) These are the results for the mock exams for History and Geography for three students A, B and C, along with the mean and standard deviation for the whole year.

	A	B	C	Mean	Standard Deviation
History	78	85	69	74	1.8
Geography	75	71	83	78	1.5

a) Work out the standardised scores for each student.
b) Which student gave the best performance overall?

Comparing Data Sets

Averages and measures of spread can be combined to compare different sets of data.

The following sets of data show the percentage results (in ascending order) for 20 students in French and English:

French: 31 35 39 40 43 43 45 47 47 48 51 55 59 62 65 65 68 71 72 78

English: 37 38 42 42 43 45 48 49 50 51 51 57 58 59 59 60 61 61 64 65

Comparing Data Sets — Which Measure is Most Useful?

The table and box plots below show some comparisons between the two sets of data.

	French	English
Mean	53.2	52
Median	49.5	51
Mode	43, 47, 65	42, 51, 59, 61
Range	47	28
Upper Quartile	65	59.5
Lower Quartile	43	44
Interquartile Range	22	15.5
Standard Deviation	13.19	8.60

FRENCH

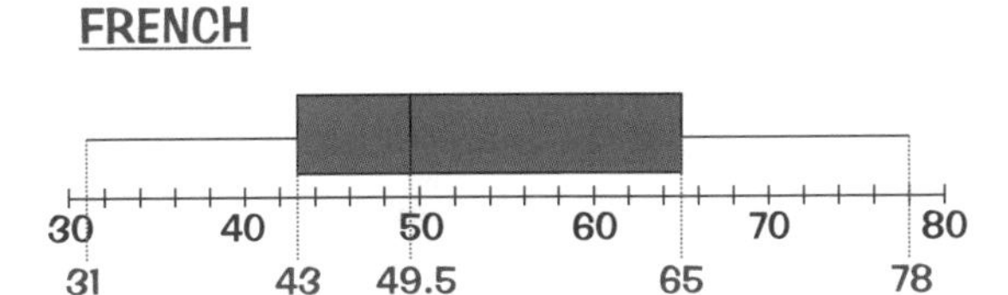

ENGLISH

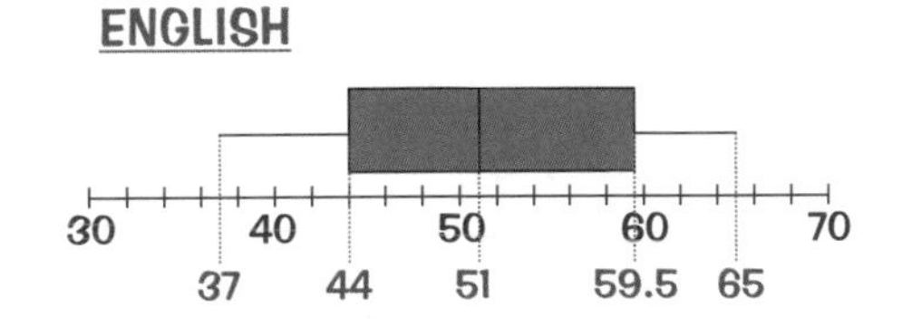

1) The box plots show that the results for English were much closer together, having a smaller range.
2) The STANDARD DEVIATIONS also show this, but that's all they show. Unlike the box plot, they don't give you any idea of the actual values.
3) The MEAN and MEDIAN are always useful to give you a quick average or central location of the data. The mode, in this case, is not much use at all.

It Can be Useful to Compare Individual Values

...but only if you're doing AQA

Higher

Standardised scores let you compare standards of performance.

EXAMPLE: Compare the top marks in French and English.

Standardised top score for French = (78 – 53.2)/13.19 = 1.88
Standardised top score for English = (65 – 52)/8.6 = 1.51

These results show that the top score for French was better than that in English — it was better in relation to the other students' performances.

The Acid Test:

Check the results in the table for French and English. When you agree with them all, look back at the data and answer this question.

1) a) What are the standardised lowest scores for French and English?
b) In which subject was the worst performance?

Summary Statistics

Simple Index Numbers — Just Percentages Really

Index numbers are usually used to compare price changes over time.
The values are compared to the values in a particular year — known as the base year.

$$\text{INDEX NUMBER} = \frac{\text{value}}{\text{value in base year}} \times 100$$

The value in the base year always has an index of 100 (meaning 100%)

EXAMPLE: *The table below shows the price of a house over three years. 2001 is the base year. Find the index number for 2003.*

Year	2001	2002	2003
House Price	£148,000	£167,000	£174,000

$$\text{Index number for 2003} = \frac{174\,000}{148\,000} \times 100 = 117.6$$

Higher

Chain Base Numbers are Index Numbers from Year to Year

CHAIN BASE NUMBERS are index numbers which show how values change from year to year.
They always use the PREVIOUS YEAR as the base year.

Weighted Index Numbers Take Proportions Into Account

E.g. a dried fruit mixture contains apricots and prunes in the ratio 5:2. If the price of apricots or prunes goes up, then so will the price of the mixture. BUT... a rise in the price of apricots will have more effect on the price of the mixture than a rise in the price of prunes.

WEIGHTED INDEX NUMBERS take the difference in importance into account.
And there's a lovely formula for it too —

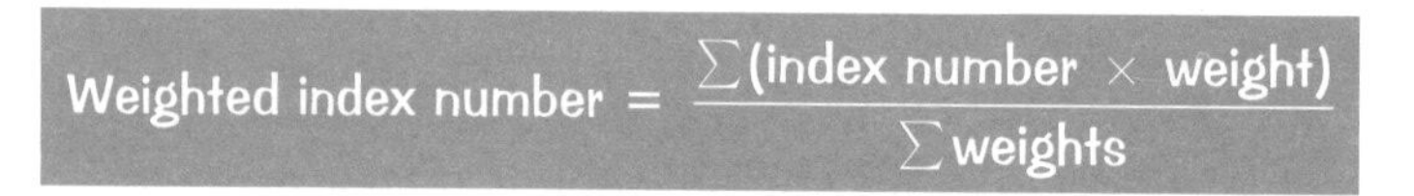

EXAMPLE: *Every year a school holds a cheese and wine party and always buys the same amount of cheese and wine — 5 kg of cheese and 10 cases of wine. Using the table on the right, calculate the weighted index number for 2003 using 2000 as the base year.*

	2000	2003	Weight
Cost of Cheese (per kg)	£3.40	£3.70	5
Cost of Wine (per case)	£42	£39	10

$$\text{Cheese index number} \times \text{weight} = \left(\frac{3.7}{3.4} \times 100\right) \times 5 = 544.12$$

$$\text{Wine index number} \times \text{weight} = \left(\frac{39}{42} \times 100\right) \times 10 = 928.57$$

$$\text{So, the WEIGHTED INDEX NUMBER} = \frac{544.12 + 928.57}{5 + 10} = 98.18 \text{ (2 d.p.)}$$

THE RETAIL PRICE INDEX (RPI) IS A WEIGHTED INDEX:
It shows changes in the cost of living for an average person or family. Every month, the prices of loads of items (the same ones each month) are combined to get a weighted index number. The weightings are chosen to show the spending habits of an average family. As stuff gets more expensive, this index number gets higher and higher.

The Acid Test:

LEARN what the different index numbers mean and how to work them out.

1) In 2004, 1 kg of cheese costs £4.00 and a case of wine costs £37. Find the weighted index number for 2004 using 2000 as the base year.

See the above example for the 2000 costs.

Summary Statistics

This page is for AQA only.

Crude Rates Tell You How Many In Every 1000

CRUDE DEATH RATES are the number of deaths per thousand of the population.
CRUDE BIRTH RATES are the number of births per thousand of the population.

$$\text{Crude birth/death rate} = \frac{\text{number of births/deaths}}{\text{total population}} \times 1000$$

EXAMPLE: Bodbury has a population of 142 000. There were 3270 deaths there last year. What was the crude death rate in Bodbury last year?

$$\text{Crude death rate} = \frac{3270}{142\,000} \times 1000 = 23.03$$

This means that last year there were about 23 deaths for every 1000 people in Bodbury. This is okay as a rough guide to the death rate in Bodbury alone, but is not much use for comparing it with different areas. One town may be full of retirement homes — more elderly residents means the death rate is bound to be higher.

Higher

Standardised Rates are More Useful

Standardised rates take the age groups of people living in an area into consideration. This means you can compare the death rates of different places fairly.

There's a FORMULA for this too. You use something called the standard population — this is the number of people in each age group over the whole country (usually given as a percentage), which you can get from census data. First, work out the crude rate for each age group individually.

$$\text{Standardised rate} = \frac{\sum(\text{crude rate for age group} \times \text{standard population for age group})}{\sum(\text{standard population})}$$

EXAMPLE: The number of deaths in Bodbury and Allfit last year are recorded in the table. Calculate the standardised death rate in both places.

	Bodbury		Allfit		Standard Population
Age Group	Population	No. of Deaths	Population	No. of Deaths	
< 40	72,000	180	83,000	160	42
40 - 60	41,000	360	47,000	340	34
> 60	29,000	2,730	90,000	6,200	24

The standardised death rate in Bodbury

$$= \frac{\left(\frac{180\times1000}{72\,000}\times42\right)+\left(\frac{360\times1000}{41\,000}\times34\right)+\left(\frac{2730\times1000}{29\,000}\times24\right)}{42+34+24} = \frac{105+298.537+2259.310}{100} = 26.63$$

The standardised death rate in Allfit

$$= \frac{\left(\frac{160\times1000}{83\,000}\times42\right)+\left(\frac{340\times1000}{47\,000}\times34\right)+\left(\frac{6200\times1000}{90\,000}\times24\right)}{42+34+24} = \frac{80.964+245.957+1653.333}{100} = 19.80$$

This tells you that the standardised death rate in Allfit is LOWER than that in Bodbury (even though the crude death rate is higher there) so it would seem that the people of Allfit are generally healthier.

The Acid Test:

LEARN how to work out the crude and standardised rates. Then answer this question WITHOUT peeking at the formulas.

1) How does the standardised death rate of Coldwich compare to that of Allfit? Use the data of deaths in Coldwich on the right.

Age Group	Population	No. of Deaths
< 40	54,000	80
40 - 60	35,000	290
> 60	41,000	3,450

Time Series

Time series use data taken over a period of time at equal intervals to show trends.

The Trend Line is Used for Making Predictions

EXAMPLE: The following data shows the unemployment figures (in thousands) for Idleville averaged over each six-month period from January 2000 till December 2003.

	2000	2001	2002	2003
Jan - Jun	78	97	103	114
Jul - Dec	84	76	92	99

This data can be plotted on a time series graph:

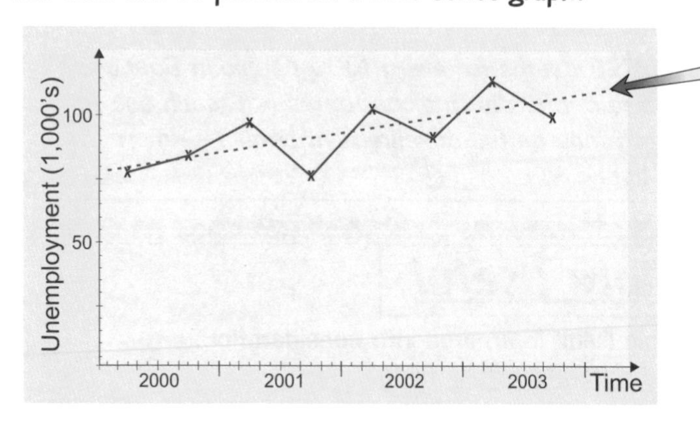

The trend line is just like a line of best fit. It's drawn through the middle of the data so the number of plotted points is roughly the same on either side of it.

This trend line can be used to predict the unemployment figures for a future date.

Moving Averages give a More Accurate Prediction

Not for AQA Foundation

A moving average "smooths out" fluctuations in the data, and lets you work out a lot more precisely where the trend line should go.

The data values from the example on unemployment figures are shown in this table. The values have been arranged in a line to make it easier to see how the moving average works.

2000	2001	2002	2003
78, 84	97, 76	103, 92	114, 99

1st average = (78+84+97+76)/4 = 83.75

2nd average = (84+97+76+103)/4 = 90

1) I'm using a 4-point moving average here. That means taking the average of each group of four consecutive data values, i.e. you'd start by taking the average of 78, 84, 97 and 76.

2) You then move along one and average the next group of values i.e. 84, 97, 76 and 103 — and so on through the data.

3) By plotting these moving averages, you can see more clearly where the trend line needs to go.

The Acid Test:

Make sure you know how to work out moving averages, then answer this question.

1) a) Work out the remaining moving averages for the unemployment data above.
b) Plot the moving averages on a graph and draw a trend line through these points.
c) Use the trend line to predict what the unemployment figure will be for Jan - Jun, 2004.

More on Time Series

Some time series graphs fluctuate in cycles. This is called seasonal variation or seasonality.
More ice creams are sold in the summer when it's hot, people spend more money at Christmas, etc.

Seasonal Variation — The Same Basic Pattern

The table below shows the quarterly profits (in £) for a lingerie department over three years.

	Jan - Mar	Apr - Jun	Jul - Sep	Oct - Dec
2001	3000	4500	4800	7100
2002	3200	4000	4900	6200
2003	3600	4800	5500	7800

The profits soared in the last quarter of each year, probably due to Christmas sales.

Plot a Trend Line using Moving Averages

The pattern repeats after every fourth point, so you should use a 4-point moving average. That means taking the average of each group of four consecutive data values.

1st moving av. = (3000 + 4500 + 4800 + 7100)/4 = 4850
...and the rest:
4900, 4775, 4800, 4575, 4675, 4875, 5025, 5425.

Now, plot the moving averages on the graph — the line of best fit through these points is the TREND LINE.

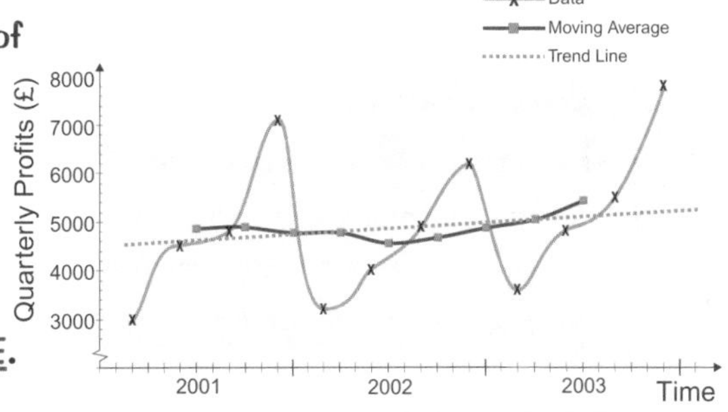

Seasonal Effect — The Gap Between Real Value and Trend Line

The difference between a real value and the value taken from the trend line is known as the SEASONAL EFFECT.

REAL value — *TREND LINE value (read this off the graph)*

E.g. The seasonal effect for the 4th quarter in 2001 is £7100 – £4700 = £2400 ← *SEASONAL EFFECT*

If you're doing Edexcel, you don't need this last bit.

The AVERAGE SEASONAL EFFECT is the mean of all the seasonal effects for the same point in each cycle. In the example, the average seasonal effect could be calculated for each quarter.

So, the average seasonal effect for the 1st quarter is:

[(3000 – 4500) + (3200 – 4800) + (3600 – 5000)]/3 = –£1500

You can use this average to make more accurate PREDICTIONS.
The predicted sales profit is the value taken from the trend line PLUS the average seasonal effect.

So, the predicted sales profit for the 1st quarter in 2004 is £5250 – £1500 = £3750

The Acid Test:

LEARN how to work out the seasonal effect. Then answer this question WITHOUT peeking at the method.

1) The table shows the quarterly electricity bills (in £) for the Green family over the last three years.

	Jan - Mar	Apr - Jun	Jul - Sep	Oct - Dec
2001	280	180	140	210
2002	260	150	150	230
2003	250	160	140	220

a) Plot these points on a time series graph.
b) Calculate and plot the moving averages on the same graph.
c) Draw the trend line for the moving averages.
d) What is the average seasonal effect for the 4th quarter?
e) Predict their bill for the 4th quarter of 2004.

Higher Higher Higher Higher Higher Higher

Quality Assurance

Quality Assurance is Making Sure Products Turn out Okay

People can make mistakes, and machinery can stop working properly. Quality assurance is about making sure that certain measured values stay as close as possible to target values.

QUALITY ASSURANCE METHOD:

1) Take a small sample from the production line at REGULAR intervals.
2) Measure each product and find an AVERAGE measurement for the whole sample. This is usually the mean or median — but it depends on what you're checking.
3) Plot the averages against the time the samples were taken.
4) Look for any TRENDS or OUTLIERS that suggest something's wrong.
5) If all's not well, stop production and do something about it.

EXAMPLE: A protractor manufacturer wants to be sure that his instruments are made accurately.

1) *He takes 10 protractors each hour and uses them to measure a known angle of 40°. He finds the average of each group of ten.*
2) *He plots each average against the time he took the sample.*
3) *All the averages are within one degree of the target value. There's nothing to suggest that anything is wrong.*
4) *No need to do anything — all seems to be okay.*

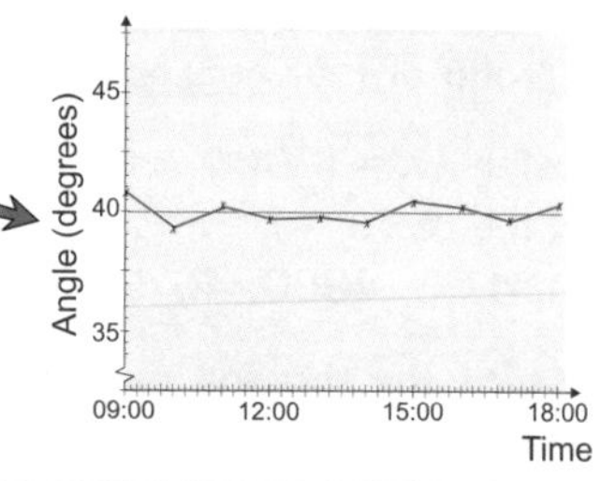

Quality Assurance Graphs — When is Something Wrong?

The graphs below show other possible results from the protractor factory.

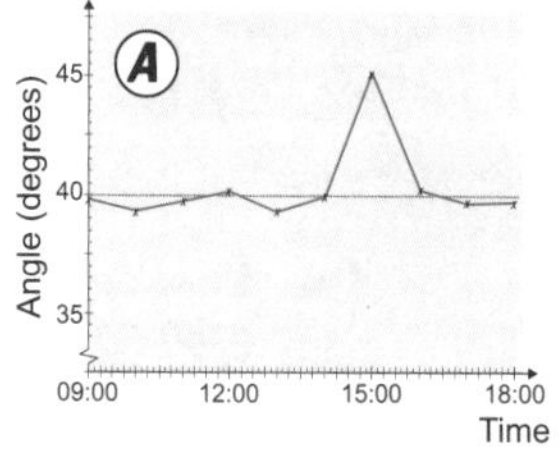

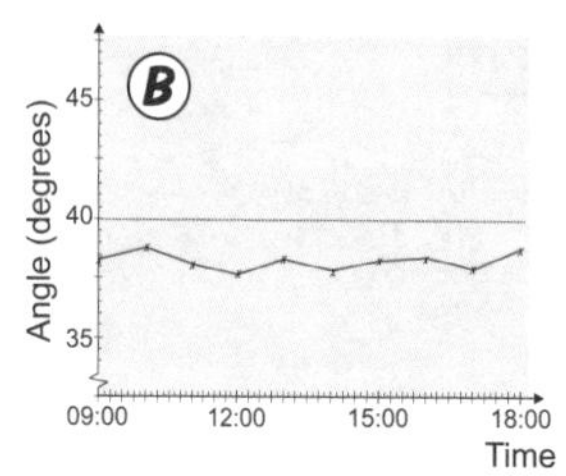

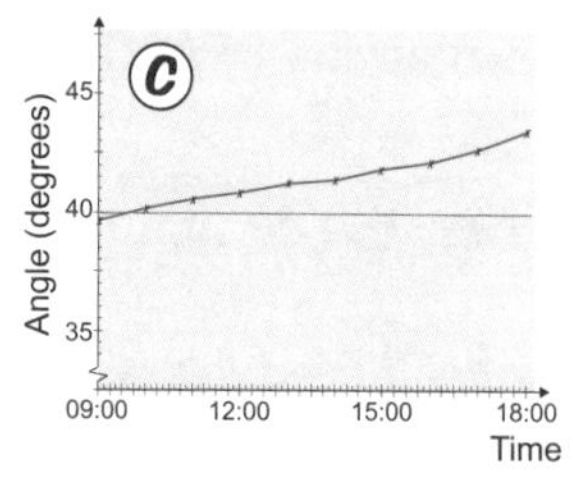

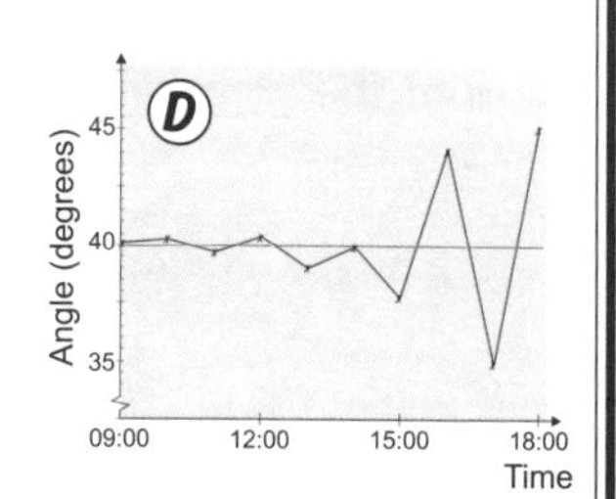

A — one average is an outlier. The machine needed to be checked at 15:00.

B — all averages are below the target value. The machine's faulty and probably needs resetting.

C — the averages are moving away from the target value. The machine needs checking.

D — the mean of the averages is okay, but the variability is increasing. The machine needs checking.

The Acid Test:

Learn the five steps in the Quality Assurance method.

1) A factory production line makes trousers with an 80 cm inside leg. As a quality control check, samples were taken each hour on two consecutive days and the median lengths recorded.

a) Plot Monday's averages against time.

b) The results were checked at the end of the day. Should any action have been taken?

c) Plot Tuesday's averages against time. Was any action required on Tuesday?

	10:00	11:00	12:00	13:00	14:00	15:00	16:00	17:00
Mon	81	80	82	79	83	82	81	83
Tues	79	79	81	80	81	79	80	80

Correlation

You might want to find out whether or not two variables are related in any way — e.g. are GCSE Statistics exam marks related to the amount of revision a person does? Hmmmmm...

Scatter Diagrams Show Whether Two Variables are Related

SCATTER DIAGRAMS are graphs with two variables plotted against each other (bivariate data).

When you're drawing a scatter diagram:

1) The SCALE doesn't have to be the same on both axes, so pick 'easy to use' scales for both axes. Try not to use a scale that leaves you guessing where to plot a point.
2) PLOT the points carefully (a sharp pencil helps). Check that the number of plotted points equals the number of pairs of variables.

Correlation — Can you See a Line Forming?

Drawing "lines of best fit" can help you see the correlation (see p.57).

CORRELATION is just a fancy term for how closely related two things are.

A

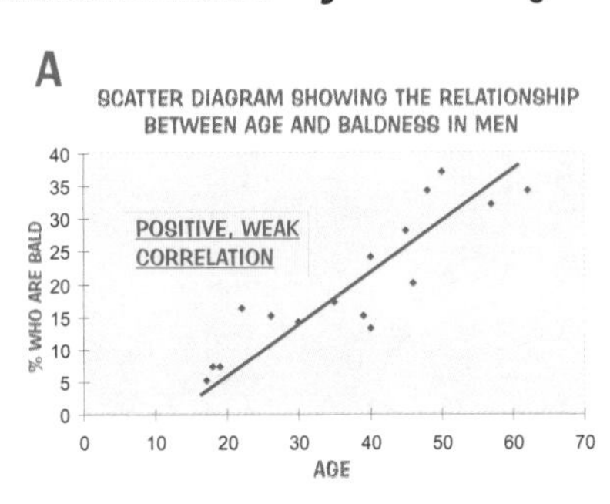

B

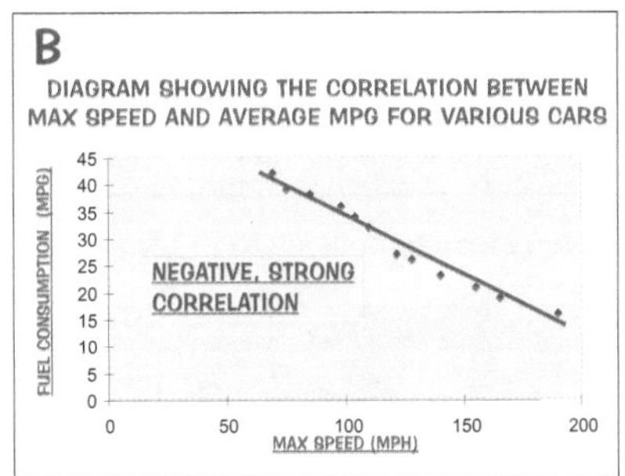

C

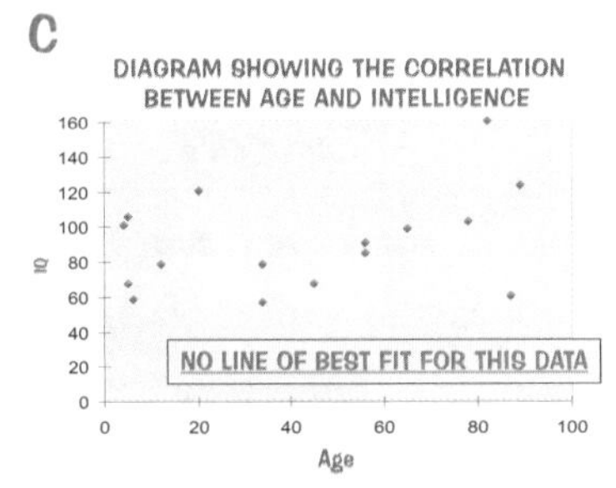

These scatter diagrams show three different types of correlation:

A shows positive correlation — as one variable increases, the other one does too.
B shows negative correlation — as one variable increases, the other one decreases.
C shows no correlation — the variables aren't linearly related. (There might be some other relationship between them, but the scatter diagram won't tell you that.)

Strong and Weak are also words used to describe correlations. A Strong Correlation is when the points are close to the line of best fit. A Weak Correlation is when they're spread out more.

Causality — When one Variable Causes Changes in the Other

If a change in one variable CAUSES a change in the other variable, they're said to have a CAUSAL LINK, e.g. a rise in the temperature outside could cause an increase in ice cream sales. However, an increase in ice cream sales wouldn't cause the weather to improve — unfortunately.

You have to be VERY CAREFUL with causality, though. Just because there's a correlation between two things, it doesn't necessarily mean there's a causal link — there could be a third factor involved. For example, the number of pairs of sunglasses sold per week in a particular town is positively correlated with the amount of algae in a local pond. Neither one causes the other, though. Both of these increases are probably due to an increase in the amount of sunshine.

The Acid Test:

Learn everything on the page, then answer this question.

1) Describe the correlation you would expect for each of the following pairs of variables:
   i) Adult shoe size and waist size.
   ii) Hours of sunshine in a day, and hours of rain in day.
   iii) No. of power cuts and no. of candles sold.
   iv) Age and height of primary school children.

Spearman's Rank Correlation Coefficient

Spearman's rank correlation coefficient, often shortened to r_s (bit less of a mouthful) measures how closely related two sets of data are. It only works for data that can be ranked into place order, (highest to lowest or first to last) — e.g. exam marks and the number of hours spent revising.

Higher

There's a Nasty Formula for Working Out r_s

FOUR-STEP METHOD for finding r_s:

1. Rank both sets of data. For each set, give the highest value a rank of 1, the next highest a rank of 2, and so on.
2. Find the DIFFERENCE in rank (d) between the two values in each data pair.
3. Count the number of data pairs, n.
4. Use the following formula to find r_s: $r_s = 1 - \frac{6\sum d^2}{n(n^2 - 1)}$

This is on your formula sheet, so you don't need to learn it.

EXAMPLE: *Two judges awarded marks to high-board divers from six different countries as follows:*

	Aus	Bul	Ch	Den	Est	Fra
Judge Judy	5.7	4.9	6.0	6.3	5.9	5.5
Judge Dredd	5.8	5.2	5.8	6.0	6.1	5.6

Rank the marks and find *d* for each country:

	Aus	Bul	Ch	Den	Est	Fra
Judge Judy	4	6	2	1	3	5
Judge Dredd	3.5	6	3.5	2	1	5
d	0.5	0	1.5	1	2	0
d^2	0.25	0	2.25	1	4	0

Judge Dredd gave Austria and China the same mark, so they get the same rank — they share ranks 3 and 4 between them.

There are 6 data pairs, so n = 6.

$$\sum d^2 = 0.25 + 0 + 2.25 + 1 + 4 + 0 = 7.5$$

So, $r_s = 1 - \frac{6 \times 7.5}{6(6^2 - 1)} = 1 - \frac{45}{210} = 0.786$ (to 3 d.p.)

r_s is Always Between –1 and 1

Strong Negative Correlation	Weak Negative Correlation	No Correlation	Weak Positive Correlation	Strong Positive Correlation
–1.0	–0.5	0	+0.5	+1.0

Values of r_s are between –1 and +1

In the example, the Spearman's rank correlation coefficient is very close to 1. This means that the two judges were pretty much in agreement about the performance of the six divers.

The Acid Test:

Make sure you know how to work out Spearman's rank correlation coefficient, and what it means.

1) Lewis and Dee were given eight flavours of ice cream (A-H) to try and asked to give each flavour marks from one to ten, the highest being the best.

	A	B	C	D	E	F	G	H
Lewis	5	9	2	5	6	8	6	3
Dee	10	3	7	6	2	3	8	5

a) Work out Spearman's rank correlation coefficient for the data.

b) How do their tastes compare?

Working with Scatter Diagrams

If a scatter diagram shows correlation, you can draw a 'line of best fit'.

Line of Best Fit — A Straight Line Through the Data

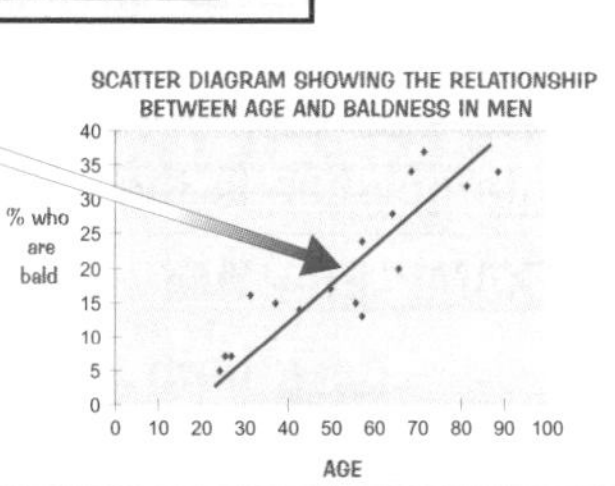

1) The LINE OF BEST FIT should run right through the MIDDLE of the plotted points, ideally through the mean of both variables, and so that it is close to as many points as possible.
2) You should end up with roughly the same number of plotted points on either side of the line.
3) The closer the points are to the line, the STRONGER the correlation.

To find the equation of the line, use $y = mx + c$

The equation of the line of best fit can be written in the form $y = mx + c$, where 'm' is the gradient and 'c' is the y-intercept (where the line crosses the y-axis).

EXAMPLE: It is widely believed in Somerset that anyone who can throw a cricket ball a long way should be able to throw a Wellington boot just as well. 20 people tested this theory and plotted the results on a scatter diagram.

1) First, find the gradient...
   Pick two points on the line, the further apart the better.
   In this case (0,0) and (30,20) look good.
   Gradient, m, is "the change in y" over "the change in x"
   So, $m = 20/30 = 2/3$
2) Next, find the y-intercept, c...
   $c = 0$, because the line passes through the origin.
3) So the equation of the line is $y = (2/3)x$.

Now you can estimate how far someone will be able to throw a welly based on how far they can throw a cricket ball (or vice versa) using the equation. So, if you can throw a cricket ball 45 m, you should be able to throw a welly $(2/3) \times 45 = 30$ m.

Non-Linear Data Lies on a Curve

If the line of best fit through the points on a graph is a curve, the relationship is non-linear. You can sometimes make this into a nice straight-line graph (which is a lot easier to analyse) by plotting y against an expression with x in (rather than just x). You'll be told in the exam what expression to use.

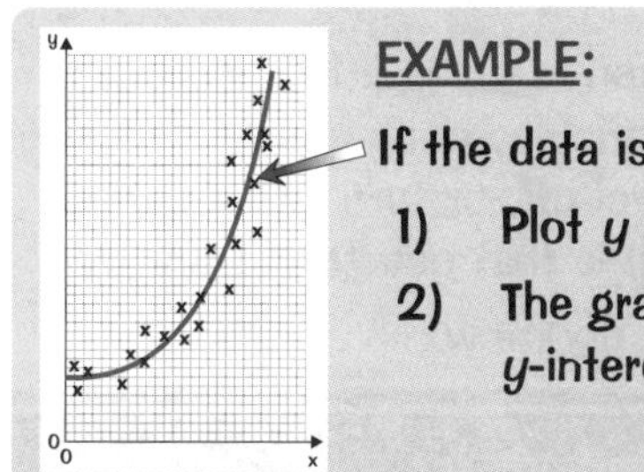

EXAMPLE:

If the data is related by $y = ax^2 + c$:

1) Plot y against x^2.
2) The gradient is a and the y-intercept is c.

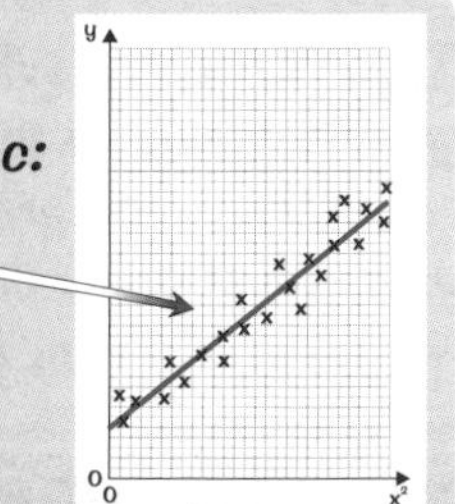

LEARN THIS TOO...
If the data is related by $y = a/x + c$
Plot y against $1/x$.
The gradient is a and the y-intecept is c.

The Acid Test:

There's some tricky stuff on this page — especially the bits about non-linear data. So make sure you know it.

1) The height of water in a water tank is measured every 30 minutes, as shown in the table.
a) Plot the points on a graph and draw a line of best fit.
b) Find the equation of the line.

Time (mins)	30	60	90	120	150	180	210	240
Height (cm)	440	420	395	365	345	330	305	280

Interpolation and Extrapolation

(This page is for AQA only) You can use the line of best fit on a scatter diagram to predict unknown values, using either interpolation or extrapolation — scary words but they're not too bad really...

Use Interpolation to Find Values Within your Data Set

Interpolation is the method you use to find a value that lies between two known values.

EXAMPLE: – This scatter diagram shows the chest and waist sizes of ten men.

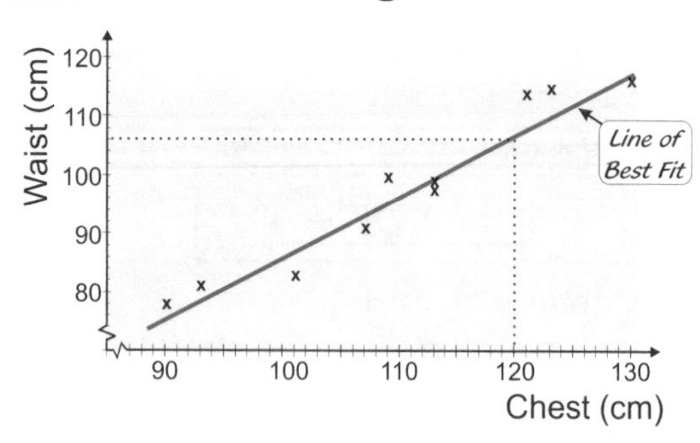

You can use the line of best fit to estimate the waist size of a man with a 120 cm chest — using interpolation.

1) Draw a vertical line from 120 on the x-axis to the line of best fit.
2) Draw a horizontal line from this point to the y-axis.
3) Read off the value — so, 106 cm is the estimate for a man's waist size if he has a chest size of 120 cm... it's as easy as that.

Interpolation tends to give fairly reliable results — so long as you get the line of best fit right.

Extrapolation Looks Beyond the Sampled Data

You can also make predictions outside of the plotted data — and this is called extrapolation.
There are two ways to do this:

1) extend the line of best fit, then find the values you're after just like you did for interpolation,
2) or, better still, use the equation of the line (see p.57).

EXAMPLE: The equation for the line of best fit in the example above is $y = 1.1x - 26$.
To estimate the waist size (y) for a man with a chest size (x) of 80 cm, just stick your value of x into the equation...

$$y = 1.1(80) - 26 = 62 \text{ cm}$$

So, you would expect a man with an 80 cm chest to have about a 62 cm waist.

BE VERY CAREFUL WITH EXTRAPOLATION. When you extrapolate, you're going into unknown territory. You have no idea what happens to the link between your variables once you go outside your data set, so you're just guessing. The graph might curve, or level off, or turn into a series of small furry animals... okay, that last one's unlikely — but the point is that you DON'T KNOW. So, it's a good plan not to try and extrapolate too far from what you do know.

The Acid Test:

Make sure you learn the methods for both interpolation and extrapolation — then try these...

1) The table shows the weekly sales of toads and bats over a nine-week period at Witchworths.

a) How many bats are they likely to sell in a week if they sell 48 toads?
b) Estimate the number of toads sold if they sold 32 bats in a week.
c) Predict how many bats they might expect to sell if they sell 180 toads in a week.

toads	80	49	38	58	68	72	46	70	59
bats	20	18	6	12	18	14	14	24	18

Estimation of Population

A population is a whole set of things being measured — it doesn't just mean the number of people living somewhere. So, make sure you learn what this term means...

Make Estimates about a Population Using Samples

Populations can sometimes be very large — often too big to be counted (e.g. the number of fish in the sea). To make estimates about a population (e.g. size, the mean, etc.) you need to use an appropriate sample that represents the whole population.

EXAMPLE: A market gardener has a field of 500 potato plants. He randomly selects 30 plants from different areas and finds the mean weight of a potato to be 120 grams.

1) From this sample, the gardener can ESTIMATE that the mean weight of each potato in his crop is 120 g.

See Section 1 for more on Sampling.

He also counts the number of potatoes in his sample and finds that each plant produces an average of 9 potatoes.

2) Using this estimate he can estimate the total population of his potato crop.
Estimated total number in crop = $9 \times 500 = 4500$ potatoes.

This method's fine, but you need to know how many units (e.g. plants) there are in the whole population — and sometimes you don't have this much information.
A different way of estimating a population size is by the method of capture and recapture (see p.21)...

Opinion Polls Tell You What People Think

Many organisations (e.g. governments, advertising agencies, etc.) find it very useful to know what people are thinking. They do this by asking the opinions of a selected sample of people, which are then used to represent the whole population — this is called an opinion poll.

EXAMPLE: A food manufacturer carried out an opinion poll of 1000 people to find out the nation's favourite flavour of crisps.
Six hundred people said their favourite flavour was Chilli Cheese.
The manufacturer used this result to estimate that Chilli Cheese is the favourite flavour of crisp for 60% of the population of Britain.

The bigger the sample, the more accurate the result. You wouldn't be able to form much of an opinion on what music the population of your town liked if you only asked 10 people — this sample size would be too small.

The Acid Test:

Learn the relationship between sample and population then answer this lovely little question...

1) 1,000,000 tourists visit London every year. The Tourist Office wanted to find out what they did during their stay and carried out an opinion poll of 200 people.
   a) The poll revealed that 30 tourists from the sample had visited Buckingham Palace. Use this result to estimate the percentage of all tourists who go to the palace.
   b) What is the approximate total number of tourists visiting the palace in a year?
   c) The poll also showed that 7 of the tourists questioned came from New Zealand. Estimate the total number of visitors to London from New Zealand in one year.

Revision Summary for Section Three

Here's the really fun page. The inevitable list of straight-down-the-middle questions to test how much you know. Remember, these questions will sort out quicker than anything else exactly what you know and what you don't. And that's exactly what revision is all about, don't forget: finding out what you don't know and then learning it until you do. Enjoy.

Keep learning the basic facts until you know them

1) What is another term for 'mean'?
2) How do you work out the mean?
3) What is the median?
4) What is the modal number of days in a month?
5) If coursework and exam results are combined to give an overall result, what kind of mean is generally required?
6) What method could you use for finding the mean of large numbers?
7) What kind of frequency distribution table would you use for continuous data?
8) For what kind of data is the mode likely to be a meaningful average?
9) Give one advantage of finding the mean over the median or mode.
10) How do you find the geometric mean?
11) What is the range of a set of data?
12) How would you work out the position of the lower quartile of a set of data?
13) How do you calculate the interquartile range?
14) What is the standard deviation a measure of?
15) What do you need to know to draw a box plot?
16) What is an outlier?
17) How do you find a standardised score?
18) What is the index number of a base year?
19) What is the difference between simple and chain base index numbers?
20) What is a crude rate?
21) What is the formula for finding the standardised rate?
22) What kind of moving average would you use for quarterly bills?
23) How do you find the seasonal effect?
24) What is the purpose of quality assurance?
25) What is the name of the graph used for bivariate data?
26) What is causality?
27) What range of values can Spearman's Rank Correlation Coefficient take?
28) What does a rank correlation of zero mean?
29) Where should a line of best fit be drawn?
30) What does the m represent in $y = mx + c$?
31) What is the difference between interpolation and extrapolation?
32) A lightbulb manufacturer wants to test the lifetime of its bulbs, so it finds the mean lifetime of a sample of 200 bulbs. Why is this sample mean only an estimate of the population mean?
33) What is an opinion poll?

Probability

Last section — woohoo! And it's probability. (sigh)

Probability is a Measure of How Likely an Event is

Some things are more likely to happen than others. The probability of any event happening is somewhere between impossible and certain.

"Even chance" means that something is equally likely to happen or not happen.

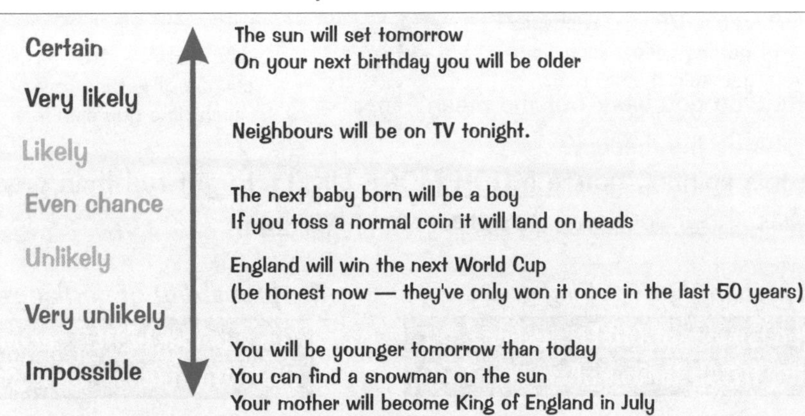

You can use Numbers instead of Words

You can put the probability of something happening on a scale of 0 to 1 — 0 means impossible and 1 means certain.

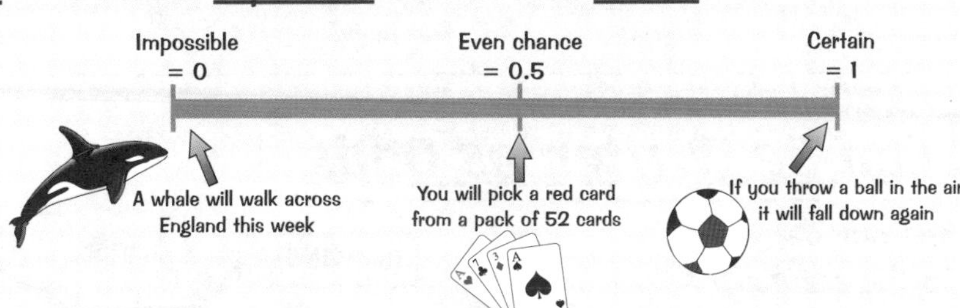

Improbable, but not impossible:

An Outcome is Just What Might Happen

An OUTCOME is something that can happen as a result of a TRIAL.
(*A trial can be anything from spinning a spinner to a horse race.*)

EXAMPLES: 1) When you toss a coin, the only possible outcomes are heads and tails. (Actually, that's not strictly true — it's *just* possible that the coin could land on its edge. The probability of that happening is so tiny that you can ignore it though.)

2) The possible outcomes of throwing a standard dice are 1, 2, 3, 4, 5 and 6.

ALWAYS THINK ABOUT ALL THE POSSIBLE OUTCOMES.

The Acid Test:

Learn all the details on this page, then turn over and write down everything you've learned.

1) List the possible outcomes for tossing a coin three times.
2) Put the probability of the following events on a scale of 0 to 1:
   a) Every light bulb will work at home as you turn them on tonight.
   b) You will clean your teeth twice today.
   c) You will get a grade C or higher in GCSE Statistics.

Probability

Spinners, odds and sinking yachts — that's the stuff of probability.

Equally Likely — the Same Chance of Each Happening

If you spin this spinner, it's EQUALLY LIKELY that you'll get yellow or green.

There's a 4/8 = 0.5 chance of getting yellow each time you spin the spinner...

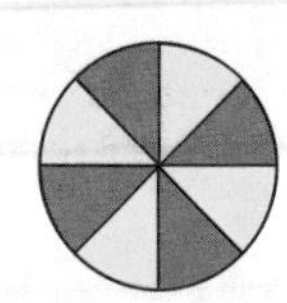

...and there's a 4/8 = 0.5 chance of getting green each time you spin it.

With this spinner, you're MUCH MORE LIKELY to get red than green. Red has three sections, but green only has one.

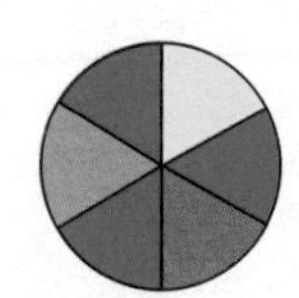

The probability of getting green is:

$$\frac{\text{The number of GREEN sections}}{\text{The TOTAL number of sections}} = \frac{1}{6}$$

The probability of getting red is:

$$\frac{\text{The number of RED sections}}{\text{The TOTAL number of sections}} = \frac{3}{6} = \frac{1}{2}$$

Remember — Probabilities ALWAYS Add up to One

For the second spinner the probability of getting:

green is $\frac{1}{6}$
yellow is $\frac{1}{6}$
blue is $\frac{1}{6}$
red is $\frac{3}{6}$

$\frac{1}{6} + \frac{1}{6} + \frac{1}{6} + \frac{3}{6} = \frac{6}{6} = 1$

Probabilities Can Be Written as Odds

Higher

Odds are the ratio of the number of favourable outcomes to the number of unfavourable outcomes.

EXAMPLE: *Four names are put in a hat. The person whose name is drawn will win a year's supply of bacon. The odds of each person winning are 1:3. The odds of each of them NOT winning are 3:1.*

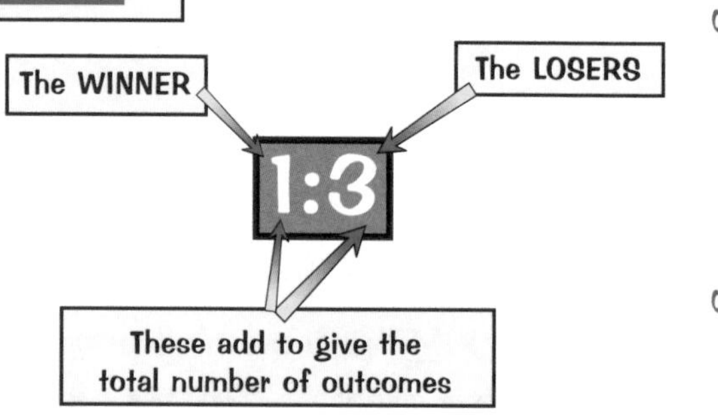

Probabilities Are Used To Assess Risk

Insurance companies use probabilities to decide how likely you are to make a claim. This is risk assessment. They'll use this information to decide how much to charge you.

EXAMPLE: *If you want insurance against your yacht sinking, the insurance company will look at how many yachts like yours sink each year and compare it to the total number of yachts like yours.*

$$\text{Estimated probability of your yacht sinking} = \frac{\text{number of yachts that sink}}{\text{total number of yachts}}$$

They'll also take into account the amount of money they'll need to pay out if your yacht does sink.

The Acid Test:

Learn how to calculate simple probabilities and how to write them as odds. Turn over and write it all down.

1) In a race between 5 pink poodles and 3 green poodles, all of equal fitness, what is the probability of a pink poodle winning?

Sample Space and Venn Diagrams

Things are pretty straightforward when you've only got one event to worry about.
It's when you get two or more things happening that things start to get stressful.

A Sample Space is a List of ALL Possible Outcomes

If you throw a normal dice, there are 6 possible outcomes.

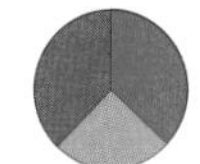

If you spin a spinner with 3 colours, there are 3 possible outcomes.

Throwing the dice AND spinning the spinner gives 18 (6×3) different combinations altogether (since any number on the dice could come up with any colour on the spinner).
A list of these 18 outcomes is called a SAMPLE SPACE. Luckily, there's some easy ways to work out what these outcomes can be.

1 Use a Sample Space Diagram to List all the Outcomes

A sample space diagram is basically a posh name for a table.
If you use one, you're less likely to miss out any outcomes.

This table uses columns for the spinner outcomes and rows for the dice. It doesn't matter which way round you do it though.

	Red	Blue	Green
1	1R	1B	1G
2	2R	2B	2G
3	3R	3B	3G
4	4R	4B	4G
5	5R	5B	5G
6	6R	6B	6G

If you're doing EDEXCEL FOUNDATION you can skip the rest of the page.

2 Cartesian Grids are Graphs of Sample Space Diagrams

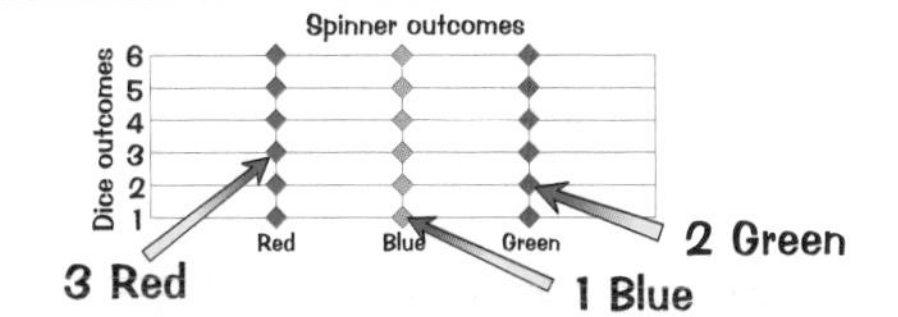

To draw one of these, use a grid with each line showing an outcome. There's a different combination at each point where the lines cross.

3 A Venn Diagram Shows Sample Space Too

The Venn diagram on the right has spaces for every combination of items from the menu. It's filled in below for 32 pupils.
Where the circles overlap, the pupils had both or all three things.

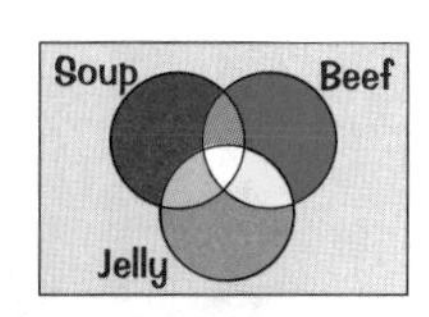

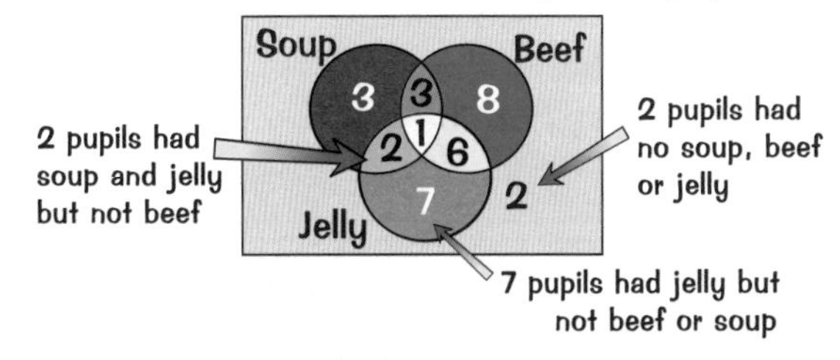

So, the total number who had JELLY was 16.
Of these: 7 had JELLY but NOT beef or soup,
2 had SOUP AND JELLY (no beef),
6 had BEEF AND JELLY (no soup),
1 had SOUP, BEEF AND JELLY.

If you add up all the numbers you get the TOTAL NUMBER OF PUPILS — 32.

YOU CAN USE VENN DIAGRAMS TO WORK OUT PROBABILITIES

You might be asked to work out the probabilities of certain outcomes using a Venn diagram. Here's a few examples. The probability of a randomly chosen pupil having had...

... JELLY is: $\frac{\text{Total number having had jelly}}{\text{Total number of pupils}} = \frac{16}{32} = \frac{1}{2}$

... SOUP AND BEEF is: $\frac{\text{Total number having had soup and beef}}{\text{Total number of pupils}} = \frac{4}{32} = \frac{1}{8}$

The Acid Test:

1) Set up a Cartesian grid to list the possible outcomes of tossing a coin and randomly choosing one day next week to go shopping.
2) Using the Venn diagram above, what is the probability of someone chosen at random having had soup?

Expected and Relative Frequencies

Expected Frequency — How Many Times It's Likely to Happen

Once you know the probability of something happening, you can predict how many times it will happen in a certain number of trials, e.g. the number of sixes you could expect if you threw a dice 20 times. This prediction is called the EXPECTED FREQUENCY.

EXPECTED FREQUENCY = NUMBER OF TIMES you are going to do something (the number of trials) × The PROBABILITY of the outcome happening

EXAMPLE: What is the expected frequency of heads when you toss a standard coin 200 times?

1. *First work out the probability of the outcome happening.*
   There are two possible outcomes when you toss a coin — it's either going to land heads up or tails up, and either is equally likely. So the probability of getting heads is 0.5.
2. *Now use the formula for expected frequency.* Expected Frequency = 200 × 0.5 = 100
   (200 = *tosses*; 0.5 = *probability of heads*)

So, the EXPECTED FREQUENCY would be 100 heads (out of 200 tosses).

The Results Might be Different from the Expected Frequency

The expected frequency tells you the most likely number of times something will happen — but if you test it you'll probably get slightly different results. Often the easiest way to compare your actual results with the predicted results (i.e. the expected frequencies) is to draw a graph.

EXAMPLE: You are asked to investigate how the expected frequency of each number on a standard dice compares to the actual frequencies you get when you throw the dice 60 times.

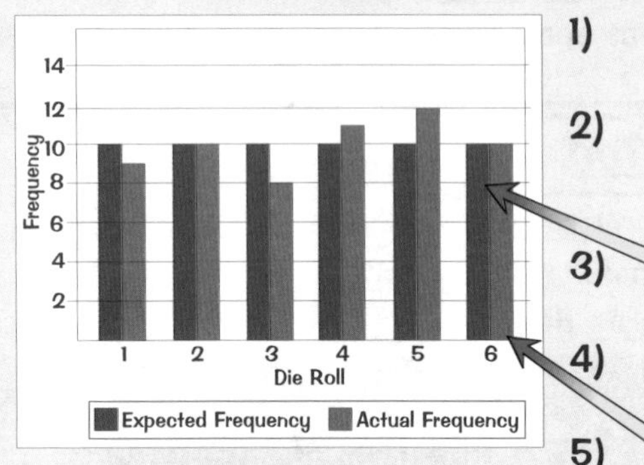

1) There are six sides on the dice and each is equally likely to come up, so the probability of getting each number is 1/6.
2) If you throw the dice 60 times, the EXPECTED FREQUENCY of each number is 1/6 × 60 = 10 (i.e. in your test you expect to get each number 10 times).
3) Draw columns on the graph to show these expected frequencies.
4) Throw the dice 60 times and record the actual number of times each number is thrown.
5) Draw these actual frequencies on the graph.

The actual frequencies are quite close to the expected frequencies, but not exactly the same.

Relative Frequency — A Way of Working Out Probabilities

The probability of getting heads on a coin toss is 0.5 — there are only two outcomes, heads and tails, which are both equally likely. But what if the coin is biased in some way? Then you don't know what the probabilities are. This is where Relative Frequency comes in. To estimate the probabilities, you carry out an experiment over and over again, then put the results into this handy formula:

$$\text{Probability of something happening (relative frequency)} = \frac{\text{Number of times it happens in experiment (or survey)}}{\text{Number of trials in experiment (or survey)}}$$

The more trials there are, the more accurate the probability.

EXAMPLE: A biased coin is tossed 20 times and 15 heads recorded. Relative frequency of heads = 15/20 = 0.75. So an estimate of the probability of getting heads with this coin is 0.75.

The Acid Test:

This stuff will get you easy marks in the exam — so make sure you learn it...

1) If you throw a standard dice 24 times, how many 4s would you expect to get?
2) a) What is the probability of picking an ace at random from a standard pack of 52 cards?
   b) If all of the cards are dealt to two players, how many aces could each player expect to get?

Probability Laws

This page deals with "either/or" probabilities, and there are two lovely laws to learn.

Mutually Exclusive Events Can't Happen Together

When two events can't happen at the same time, they are MUTUALLY EXCLUSIVE. You can use the ADDITION LAW to find the probability of either one or the other of these events happening.

$$P(A \text{ or } B) = P(A) + P(B)$$

The probability of A or B is equal to the probability of A plus the probability of B.

Example: You throw a dice once. What's the probability of rolling a 2 or a multiple of 3?

The probability of rolling a 2 is $^1/_6$
The probability of rolling a multiple of 3 is $^2/_6$ (because you can throw a 3 or a 6).
The events are mutually exclusive, so P(getting a 2 or a multiple of 3) = $\frac{1}{6}+\frac{2}{6}=\frac{3}{6}=\frac{1}{2}$

If you have more than two mutually exclusive events, you do pretty much the same thing.
You always just ADD the probabilities of each event to find the probability of one of them happening.
For example, for four mutually exclusive events: P(A or B or C or D) = P(A) + P(B) + P(C) + P(D)

Use The General Addition Law For Non-Mutually Exclusive Events

Higher

You need to use this when more than one event can happen together. You don't want to count the overlap twice, so you have to take it away — simple as that.

$$P(A \text{ or } B) = P(A) + P(B) - P(A \text{ and } B)$$

Example: You throw a dice. What's the probability of rolling a multiple of 2 or a multiple of 3?

The probability of throwing a multiple of 2 is $^3/_6$ because you could get a 2, 4 or 6.
The probability of throwing a multiple of 3 is $^2/_6$ because you could get a 3 or 6.
Rolling a six has been counted twice (since it's a multiple of 2 and a multiple of 3),
so you need to take away the probability of rolling a six ($^1/_6$).

So the answer is: $\frac{3}{6}+\frac{2}{6}-\frac{1}{6}=\frac{4}{6}=\frac{2}{3}$.

Exhaustive Events — at least One of them Must Happen

Events are EXHAUSTIVE if together they include all the possible outcomes
— so at least one of the events MUST happen.

Example: "You draw a card randomly from a standard pack of 52 playing cards.
What's the probability of picking a spade, a heart, a diamond or a club?"

Here, the four events are "picking a spade", "picking a heart", "picking a diamond" and "picking a club".
There are no other possibilities, so the probability of one of the 4 events happening must be 1.

The Probabilities of Exhaustive Mutually Exclusive Events Always Add up to 1

If you add together the probabilities of exhaustive mutually exclusive events, you ALWAYS get 1.
So the probability of any event is *1 minus the probability of all the other possible events.*
For example, the probability of picking a spade, heart or club from a pack of cards is 1 minus the probability of picking a diamond.

The Acid Test:

LEARN the details on this page, then turn over and write down everything you've learned.

1) What does "mutually exclusive" mean? 2) Write down the General Addition Law.

Probability Laws

Now we move on to probabilities with "and" in them, and two more laws for you. Exciting stuff, eh?

Independent Events are Unconnected

Two events are INDEPENDENT if one has no effect on the other.

Example: You toss a coin and then pick a card from a pack. What's the probability of the coin showing heads, and the card being a heart?

It doesn't matter which way the coin lands — it won't affect the card you pick out of the pack, so the two events are independent. The possible results are shown in this sample space diagram:

	Clubs	Diamonds	Hearts	Spades
Heads	H, C	H, D	H, H	H, S
Tails	T, C	T, D	T, H	T, S

There are 8 possible outcomes, so the probability of getting any one of the outcomes is $^1/_8$. So P(hearts and heads) = $^1/_8$.

You don't have to draw a sample space diagram and count outcomes each time, though. There's a quicker way of calculating the probability of two independent events happening — all you need to do is to multiply the probabilities of each event together. It's called the Rule of Independent Events:

CAREFUL — it only works when you've got an 'and'.

P(A and B) = P(A) × P(B)

The probability of A and B is equal to the probability of A times the probability of B.

So the above example can be worked out by saying: "The probability of picking a heart is $^1/_4$, and the probability of the coin showing heads is $^1/_2$. So P(hearts and heads) = $\frac{1}{4} \times \frac{1}{2} = \frac{1}{8}$."

By the way, it doesn't matter how many events there are as long as they're independent — you just keep multiplying to find out the probability of them all happening. So, if there are four, the Rule of Independent Events would look like this: P(A and B and C and D) = P(A) x P(B) x P(C) x P(D).

Conditional Probability is a Bit Different

Higher

Sometimes the probability of the second event depends on the outcome of the first. This is called Conditional Probability, and to tackle it, you need to use the General Multiplication Law:

P(A and B) = P(A) × P(B given that A occurs)

This just means you've got to work out how event A affects event B. You might see this phrase shortened to P(B|A).

Example: A basket of fruit contains 2 apples and 4 pears. If two fruits are picked out at random, what's the probability that they're both pears?

The chance of picking out a pear first is $^4/_6$. You then have only 5 pieces of fruit left in the basket. The probability of picking a pear, given that you have already picked a pear, is $^3/_5$.

So the probability of picking out two pears is: $\frac{4}{6} \times \frac{3}{5} = \frac{12}{30} = \frac{2}{5}$.

The Acid Test:

LEARN all the details on this page, and make sure you understand the examples.

1) Write down the Rule of Independent Events and the General Multiplication Law.
2) What is the probability of throwing a 6 on a standard dice and then rolling an even number?
3) What are the chances of successively picking 2 aces at random from a pack of cards, given that you don't replace the first card?

Tree Diagrams

Tree Diagrams are an easy way of making sure you don't make a mistake when you're using the multiplication laws. They're bound to come in useful in the Exam.

For Probability Questions Use a Tree Diagram

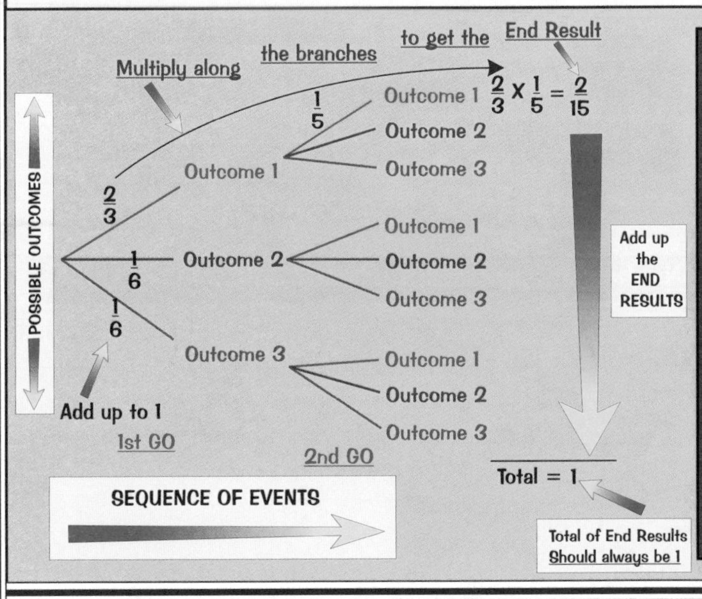

1) *Always MULTIPLY ALONG THE BRANCHES* (as shown) to get the END RESULTS.
2) *On any set of branches which all meet at a point*, the numbers must always ADD UP TO 1.
3) *Check that your diagram is correct* by making sure the End Results ADD UP TO ONE.
4) *To answer any question*, simply ADD UP THE RELEVANT END RESULTS (see below).

A likely Tree Diagram Question

This example shows you how the information in a question can be magically transformed into a tree diagram.

Example: A skier is twice as likely to fall on used snow as freshly fallen snow. On freshly fallen snow, she falls on one tenth of her runs down the slope. Snow is likely to fall every other day at the ski slope. What's the chance of the skier falling on her first run of a given day?

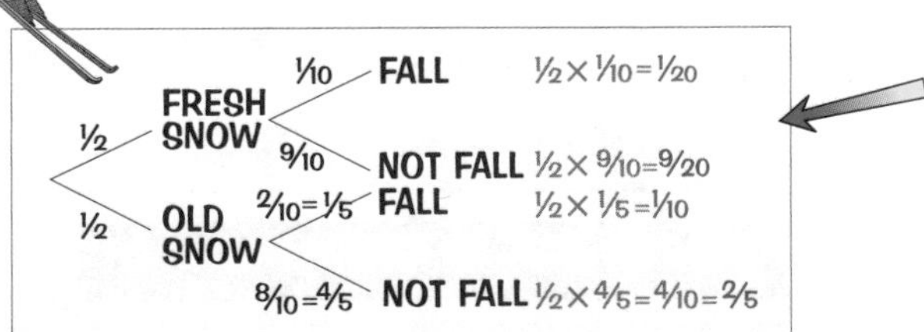

Once the tree diagram is drawn, all you need to do to answer the question is select the RELEVANT END RESULTS and then ADD THEM TOGETHER:

$$\frac{1}{20} + \frac{1}{10} = \frac{3}{20}$$

P(at least 1) = 1 – P(none)

For example: "A woman has four children. Find the probability that *at least* one of them is a girl, assuming that boys and girls are equally likely."

"At least one girl" means "1 girl", "2 girls", "3 girls" or "4 girls", which could take a while to work out. It's easier to work out P(no girls) and subtract the answer from 1.

P(no girls) = P(boy) × P(boy) × P(boy) × P(boy) = ½ × ½ × ½ × ½ = 1/16
So, P(at least one girl) = 1 – 1/16 = 15/16.

The Acid Test:

Tree diagrams are really important. Make sure you know everything about them.

1) In the 'skier' example above, work out the probability of the skier not falling on her first run of a given day.
2) The probability of a daily train service arriving late on any given day is 1/3. What is the probability of it being late at least once over a five-day period?

Discrete Probability Distributions

Uniform distribution — not wearing your tie around your neck and your trousers on your legs.

Higher

Discrete Uniform Distribution — Equal Chances

If everything is fair and you randomly pull a card from a pack, you have an equal chance of getting an ace, 2, 3, 4, 5, 6, 7, 8, 9, 10, jack, queen or king. In each case the probability is $^1/_{13}$.

If there are only a certain number of equally likely outcomes, you have a DISCRETE UNIFORM DISTRIBUTION.

A graph of the probability of each outcome looks like this:

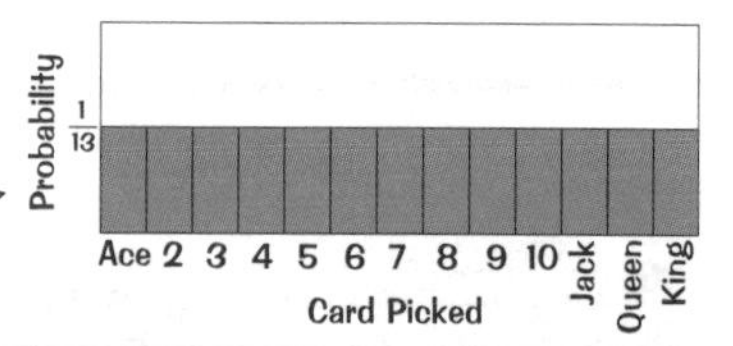

You get a DISCRETE UNIFORM DISTRIBUTION when the probability of each outcome is EQUAL.

Binomial Distribution — Two Mutually Exclusive Outcomes

Some trials only have two possible outcomes, e.g.

Toss a coin and it will be HEADS or TAILS.
Next year will be a LEAP YEAR or NOT A LEAP YEAR.

When this is true, you can use the binomial distribution to work out the probability of a certain overall outcome from n trials, e.g. a coin landing on heads 4 times out of 10 tosses.

Imagine you're tossing a fair coin. Call the probability of getting heads p and the probability of not getting heads (i.e. getting tails) q. Heads and tails are equally likely, so p = 0.5 and q = 0.5.

If you toss the coin TWICE (i.e. you carry out 2 trials) there are 4 outcomes altogether *(but 2 of these (T, H and H, T) are really the same, so there's actually only 3 different combinations).*

	Heads	Tails
Heads	H, H	T, H
Tails	H, T	T, T

The probabilities of the outcomes from these two trials are:

$P(H,H) = p \times p = p^2$, $P(H,T) = p \times q = pq$, $P(T,H) = q \times p = pq$, $P(T,T) = q \times q = q^2$.

Add these together and you get... $p^2 + 2pq + q^2$ ...which is the expansion of $(p + q)^2$.

The probability of getting two heads. The probability of getting one head and one tail.

For THREE TOSSES the result is: $p^3 + 3p^2q + 3pq^2 + q^3$ which is the expansion of $(p + q)^3$.

So, the probability of getting 2 heads and a tail is $3p^2q = 3(0.5)^2(0.5) = 0.375$

For n trials, the probabilities of the outcomes are given by the expansion of $(p + q)^n$.

You can quickly work out the expansions using Pascal's Triangle —

e.g. the expansion of $(p + q)^6$ is
$p^6 + 6p^5q + 15p^4q^2 + 20p^3q^3 + 15p^2q^4 + 6pq^5 + q^6$

Number of Trials	Coefficients in the expansion of $(p + q)^n$	Number of Different Combinations
1	1 1	2
2	1 2 1	3
3	1 3 3 1	4
4	1 4 6 4 1	5
5	1 5 10 10 5 1	6
6	1 6 15 20 15 6 1	7
etc		etc

Each number is the sum of the two numbers above it.

You can use the binomial distribution to calculate probabilities IF:
1) There are just two mutually exclusive outcomes from each trial (e.g. heads or tails).
2) The probabilities don't change from one trial to the next [e.g. P(heads) is always 0.5].
3) Each trial is independent of the one before it.

The Acid Test:

Learn ALL the stuff on the page then check you've got it by doing the question below.

1) The probability of my gran forgetting to lock the door is ¼. Use the binomial distribution to work out the chance of her forgetting to lock the door 3 out of 5 times.

Revision Summary for Section Four

Well, it's quite *probable* that you've had enough of probability by now. Don't despair — you've nearly reached the end of the section. Just a few questions to go. Keep going through them until the probability of you getting one of them wrong is *zero*. If you can answer all these, you stand a *very good chance* of doing well in the Exam.

Keep learning the basic facts until you know them

1) Give a brief definition of the word "outcome".
2) What is the numerical probability of an event which:
   a) is certain
   b) is impossible
   c) has an even chance?
3) What is the difference between probability and odds?
4) How are probabilities used by insurance companies?
5) What is a sample space?
6) Name three ways of showing a sample space.
7) How do you work out expected frequency?
8) Will your actual results always match the expected frequency?
9) What's a good way of comparing actual results with the expected frequency?
10) What are mutually exclusive events?
11) What is meant by exhaustive events?
12) What can you say about the total probability of exhaustive mutually exclusive events?
13) What is the law that can be used to work out the probability of any one of a number of mutually exclusive events happening? Write out this law.
14) What similar law should be used for events that aren't mutually exclusive? Write out this law.
15) Give an example of two events that are independent.
16) Write out the Rule of Independent Events.
17) Give a brief description of conditional probability.
18) What law can be used to find the probability of two events happening, when the second event is conditional on the first? Write out this law.
19) Write a list of everything you need to include when drawing a tree diagram.
20) What's a useful way of tackling "at least" questions?
21) When do you get a discrete uniform distribution?
22) How can you easily find the coefficients of a binomial expansion?
23) Write out the binomial expansion in terms of p and q if there are 7 trials.

Answers

SECTION ONE — DATA COLLECTION

P1 DATA SOURCES

1) a) Unprocessed data, e.g. results of a survey compiled by you on the ages of cars from streets chosen at random from the town.
   b) E.g. a report published on a government website.
2) Here are some examples of criticisms: Car dealerships tend to deal with newer cars, so the data could be biased; you're interested in average ages of cars owned rather than those recently bought, so the data might not be relevant; the car dealerships may only deal in cars made by certain manufacturers, which could make the data biased.

P2 TYPES OF DATA

1) a) Discrete quantitative   b) Continuous quantitative
   c) Qualitative   d) Continuous quantitative
   e) Qualitative   f) Discrete quantitative

P3 CLASSIFYING DATA

1) a) Ratio   b) Rank   c) Interval   d) Categorical

P4 MORE TYPES OF DATA

1) a) 16 students   b) 2 students

P5 CENSUS DATA

1) a) The population would be all the people living on the street. Yes, as it wouldn't take too much time and effort.
   b) The population would be every 16-year-old living in the UK. Probably not, due to the size of the population.

P6 SAMPLING

1) a) Not likely to be representative.   b) Likely to be representative.

P7 SAMPLING

1) The population would be all the students who attend the school.
2) The sample frame would be a list of all the students at the school.
3) Give every student on the list a number, then use a random number generator (or a table of random numbers) to get a list of 50 different random numbers up to the number of students in the sample frame. The 50 students with these numbers would form the sample.

P8 SYSTEMATIC AND STRATIFIED SAMPLING

1) Choose a random start number between 1 and 5. Then choose every fifth person on the sample frame list starting from the start number. So if the start number was 4, you would choose the 4th, 9th, 14th, ... people from the list.
2) 10/100 of the committee of 10 should be managers — so 1 manager.
   22/100 of the committee should be middle managers — that's 2.2, so round this to 2 middle managers.
   The remaining 7 people should be shop-floor workers.

P9 CLUSTER AND QUOTA SAMPLING

1) a) Cluster sample.   b) Convenience sample.   c) Quota sample.

P10 STRENGTHS AND WEAKNESSES OF SAMPLING

1) a) Convenience sample. Quick and easy to get, but data is very likely to be biased.
   b) Systematic sample. Easy to compile the list, but if there are any patterns on the list, the data could be biased.
   c) Simple random sample. The data will be unbiased, but expensive to collect as the addresses are likely to be spread out.

P11 BIASED SAMPLES

1) a) Jim's sample is biased because he has sampled from the wrong population.
      He's sampled from fish in Windermere instead of from all the fish in the Lake District.
   b) This sample is biased because it's not random. It is an example of convenience sampling, which is non-random.

P12 PLANNING AN INVESTIGATION

1) The hypothesis is that the Yumyum bar is the favourite chocolate bar of more people in the UK than any other chocolate bar.
2) Pete's hypothesis is that some "70 gram" Yumyum bars weigh less than 70 grams.

Answers

P14 QUESTIONNAIRES

1) a) open b) closed c) closed

P15 PROBLEMS WITH QUESTIONS

1) a) This is a leading question, inviting the person to agree. A better question would be, "What do you think is the most important subject taught in schools?"
   b) This question is ambiguous. "A lot of television" can mean different things to different people.
   c) The answers to this question do not cover all possible options.
   d) People are unlikely to answer this question truthfully if the answer is no.

P16 OPINION SCALES AND RANDOM RESPONSE

1) Your question should be something along the lines of:
   How attractive do you find the person in this picture? 1 2 3 4 5
   Circle the number that most applies, where 1 means very unattractive and 5 means very attractive.

P17 INTERVIEWS

1) The disadvantage is that because Fred is politically active he may record the answers to the interview in a way that is biased towards the Stark Raving Bonkers Party.

P19 MORE ON OBTAINING DATA

1) The control group isn't part of the experiment, so it gives you a standard to compare changes in the experimental group to. You can tell if any changes in the experimental group are due to changes you have made, or would have happened anyway.
   Possible methods of selection are: Using random number tables, drawing names from a hat, stratified sampling, etc.
2) Most importantly, make sure there are no factors other than the experimental ones that might influence the results. All other variables should ideally be held constant.

P20 MATCHED PAIRS & BEFORE-AND-AFTER

1) There are other factors different, e.g. temperature, humidity, that would affect the results.

P21 CAPTURE / RECAPTURE METHOD

1) 60

P22 SIMULATION

1) There are loads of ways to do this. One way would be to generate a list of twenty random numbers and take the first two digits after the decimal point of each number you generate (unless the first digit is zero).

SECTION TWO — TABULATION AND REPRESENTATION

P24 FREQUENCY TABLES

1)

Coins	0	1	2	3	4	5
Tally	|	||	𝍸 ||	𝍸 |||	𝍸 ||||	|||
Frequency	1	2	7	8	9	3

P25 GROUPED FREQUENCY TABLES

1)

Height	$0 < h \leq 5$	$5 < h \leq 10$	$10 < h \leq 15$	$15 < h \leq 20$
Tally	||||	𝍸	||	|
Frequency	4	5	2	1

P28 SIMPLIFYING AND ANALYSING DATA

1) a)

Year	1995	1996	1997	1998	1999
Total number caught speeding	108	133	159	207	235

   b) Overall speeding has increased over the 5-year period. The increase seems to be fairly steady.

Answers

c) The breakdown of professions has been lost.

d)

Professions	1995	1996	1997	1998	1999
Teachers	16.7%	24.1%	30.2%	34.8%	35.7%
Lawyers	37.0%	34.6%	33.3%	28.5%	26.8%
Editors	25.0%	27.1%	26.4%	30.9%	33.2%
Lumberjacks	21.3%	14.3%	10.1%	5.8%	4.3%

e) ADVANTAGES include — you can see what percentage of speeders were from each profession each year. You can see how those relative percentages have changed over the five-year period.
DISADVANTAGES include — you are not shown the actual numbers of speeders any more. You can't tell whether or not overall speeding is going up or down.

2) a)

Time (s)	$14 < t \leq 14.5$	$14.5 < t \leq 15$	$15 < t \leq 15.5$	$15.5 < t \leq 16$	$16 < t \leq 16.5$	$16.5 < t \leq 17$
Frequency	0	2	1	4	2	3

b) Rounding the data to 1 decimal place affects which class some of the times are in, e.g. no snails actually broke the 15 second barrier, but the table suggests that two did.

c) You no longer know how many times were in each half of each class, e.g. you lose the fact that most times between 15 and 16 seconds were in the 15.5-16 second group.

P29 BAR AND PIE CHARTS

1)

S 104.0° G 88.0° 168.0° B
New Zealand (radius = 2 cm)

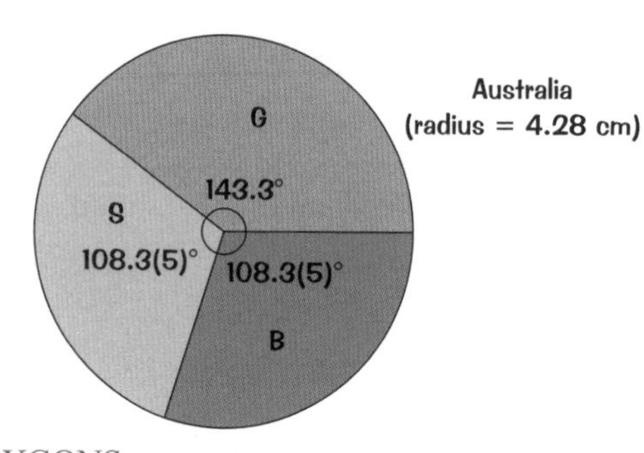

P30 DISCRETE DATA AND STEP POLYGONS

1)

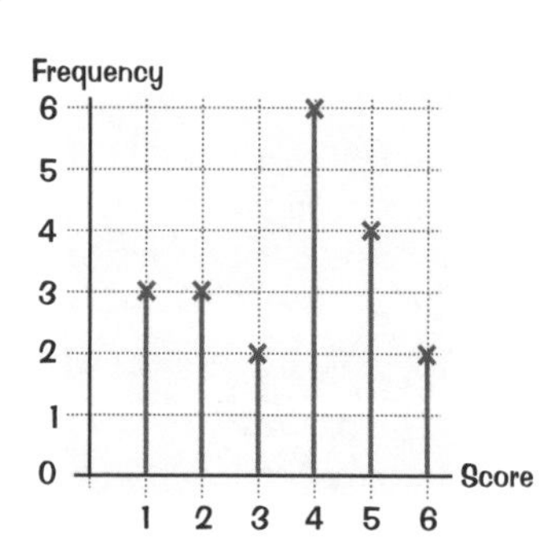

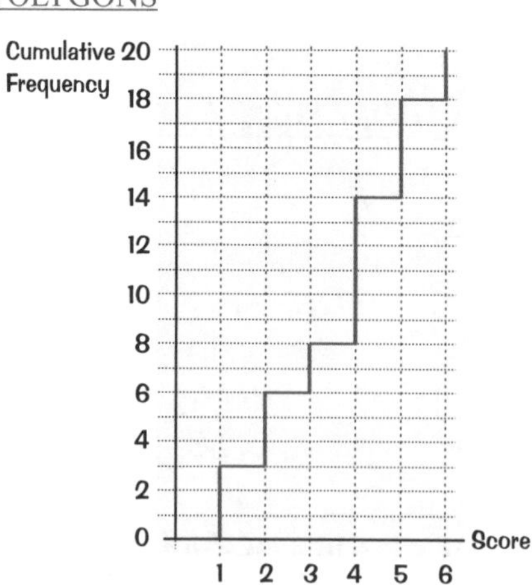

P31 OTHER DIAGRAM TYPES

1)

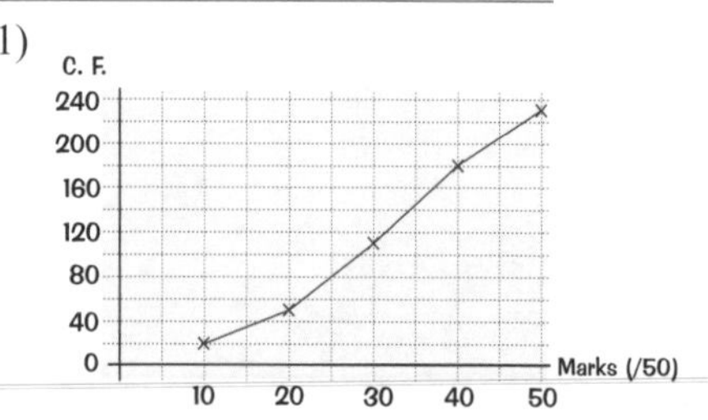

P32 OTHER DIAGRAM TYPES

1)

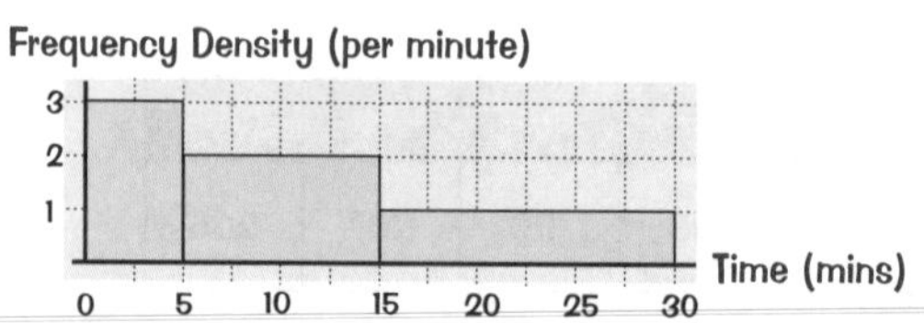

Answers

P33 STEM & LEAF DIAGRAMS AND SHADING MAPS

1) a)

CITY 1		CITY 2
8 8 4 3 2	1	6 8
8 7 6 3	2	6 7 8
9 6	3	2 2 2 3 7
1	4	2 4

key: City 1 2|1 = 12

key: City 2 1|6 = 16

b) City 1: modal distance = 18 miles. City 2: modal distance = 32 miles

c) City 1: commuting range = 41 – 12 = 29 miles. City 2: commuting range = 44 – 16 = 28 miles.

d) City 2.

P34 TRANSFORMING DATA

1) a)

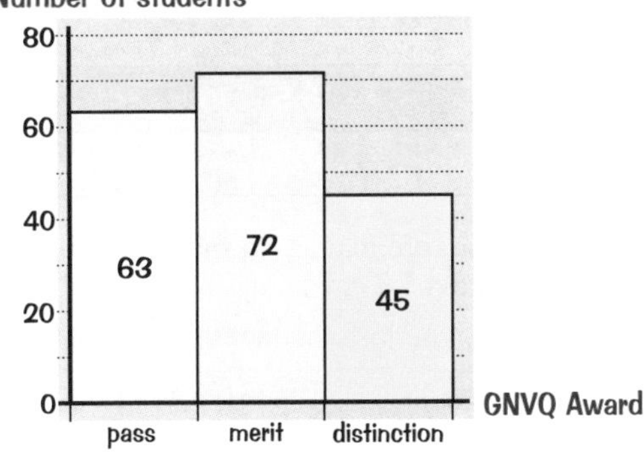

b)

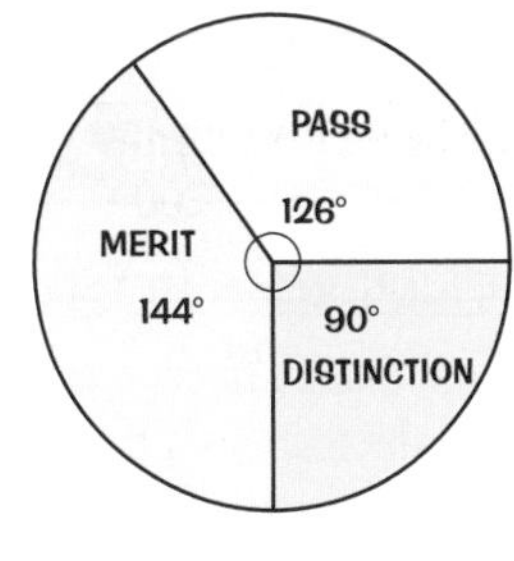

P35 FREQUENCY DISTRIBUTIONS

1) Possible answer:

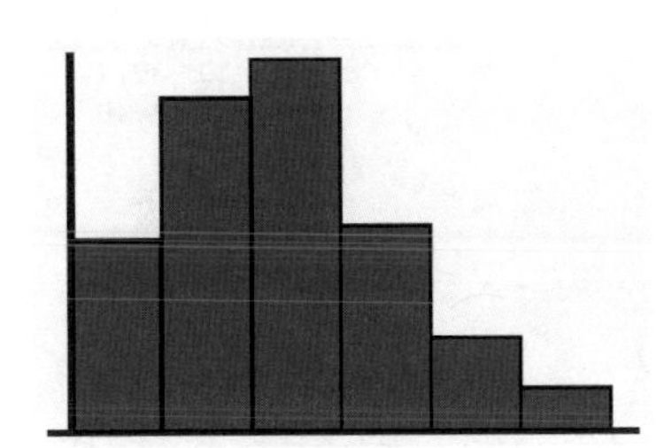

2) a) 2-3 years b) The distribution has a strong negative skew. c) 9

P36 SCATTER DIAGRAMS AND TIME SERIES

1) a) The data is seasonal with a downward trend. b) 12 months

P39 MORE DIAGRAMS, PROBLEMS AND ERRORS

1) Dia A: The *y*-axis is unlikely to be labelled correctly — there should be a key showing that the figures are in 1000s or millions of £s, or whatever. The *x*-axis years are not placed correctly — 2001 to 2003 is a two-year gap, so there should be a space 2 divisions wide between them.

   Dia B: The *y*-axis is broken — this makes the increases look a lot more dramatic than they actually are.

   Dia C: The 3-D effect is misleading — the graph appears horizontal across ability sets. This gives the impression that the sets do equally well. The symbols are so big that it would be difficult to read off average scores with any accuracy. The *y*-axis values are not equally spaced — 0-20 has the same interval as 20-35, etc.

2) Answers include:
   Neither of the axes are labelled, there is no title, the scales are not evenly spaced on either axis, one of the bars is far more brightly coloured than the other three (making it stand out more), it is unclear which part of the bar you ought to read the y-value from, the 3-D effects are generally misleading, etc.

SECTION THREE — DATA ANALYSIS

P41 MEAN, MEDIAN AND MODE

1) a) 95.7 b) 97 c) 97

2) $(60 \times 0.4) + (80 \times 0.6) = 72\%$

Answers

P 42 MEAN, MEDIAN AND MODE

1) a) 17.9 (3 s.f.) b) 18, the value in position number 22.5 c) 18

2) a)

Weight (g)	$3 < x \leq 6$	$6 < x \leq 9$	$9 < x \leq 12$	$12 < x \leq 15$
Frequency	1	9	5	3
Mid-point	4.5	7.5	10.5	13.5

Mean = 9.17 (3 s.f.)

b) 6-9, the value in position number 9.5 c) 6-9.

P43 MEAN, MEDIAN AND MODE

1) a) Median (because of the outlier 46) b) Mode c) Mean
2) 6.32 (2 d.p.)

P44 RANGE AND QUARTILES

1) The difference between the highest data value and the lowest.
2) a) 998 b) 750 c) 200 d) 850

P45 INTERQUARTILE AND INTERPERCENTILE RANGE

1) $11 - 3 = 8$
2) a) $3.1 - 1.85 = 1.25$ kg b) $P_{20} = 1.7$, $P_{80} = 3.25$ kg c) $3.25 - 1.7 = 1.55$ kg

P46 VARIANCE AND STANDARD DEVIATION

1) Variance = 4.25, Standard Deviation = 2.06 (2 d.p.) 2) 3.42 (2 d.p.) 3) 3.42 (2 d.p.)

P47 BOX AND WHISKER PLOTS

1) a)

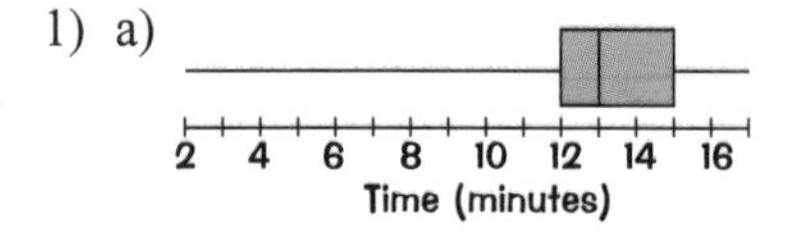

b) The value '2' is an outlier.

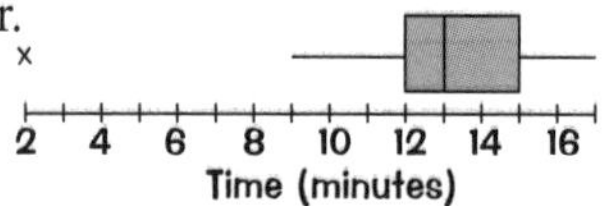

P48 STANDARDISED SCORES

1) a) The standardised scores (to 1 d.p.) in History and Geography were A, 2.2 and -2, B, 6.1 and -4.7 and C, -2.8 and 3.3
b) Student B (his/her total standardised score was the greatest).

P49 COMPARING DATA SETS

1) a) –1.68, –1.74 b) English

P50 SUMMARY STATISTICS

1) Cheese index number × weight = 588.235, wine index number × weight = 880.952
Weighted index number = 97.95 (2 d.p.)

P51 SUMMARY STATISTICS

1) Standardised death rate in Coldwich = (62.22 + 281.71 + 2019.51) ÷ (42 + 34 +24) = 23.63 (2 d.p.)
The comparative death rate in Coldwich is higher than that in Allfit.

P52 TIME SERIES

1) a) Moving averages are 92, 96.25 and 102.
b)

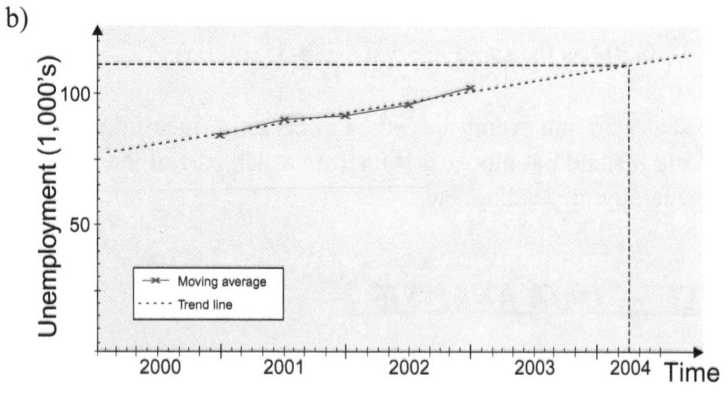

c) Trend line shown gives 112 thousand. Accept answer, consistent with graph, between 110 and 115 thousand.

Answers

P53 MORE ON TIME SERIES

1) a)

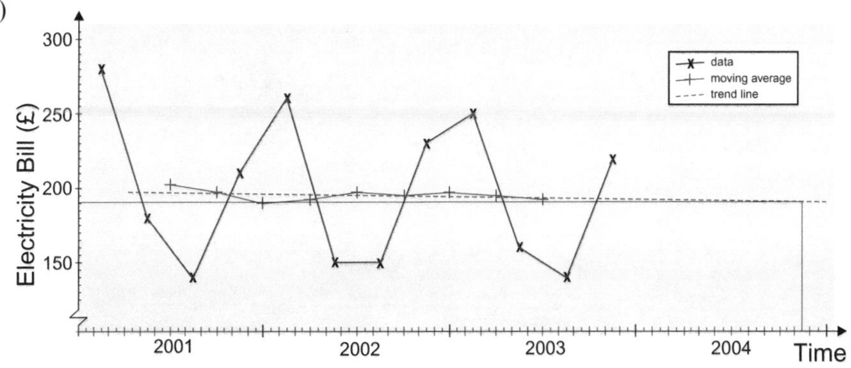

b) First point plotted between 2nd and 3rd quarters.
Points at 202.5, 197.5, 190, 192.5, 197.5, 195, 197.5, 195, 192.5.

c) Trend line may vary. Check that there are about the same number of plotted points on either side of the line.

d) £25. Trend line shown gives [(210 – 197) + (230 – 195) + (220 – 193)]/3 = 25 (accept 25 - 26).

e) 191 + 25 = £216

P54 QUALITY ASSURANCE

1) a) and c)

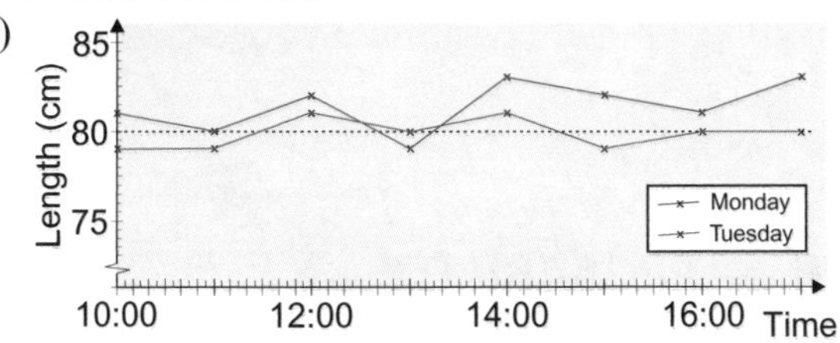

b) Most of the averages are above the target value — the production process and machinery need checking.

c) The medians were fairly evenly distributed about 80 cm, so probably no action required.

P55 CORRELATION

1) i) Weak positive correlation
ii) Moderate negative correlation
iii) Fairly strong positive correlation
iv) Fairly strong positive correlation

P56 SPEARMAN'S RANK CORRELATION COEFFICIENT

1) a) 1 – [6(124.5)]/8(63) = –0.482 (3 d.p.)

b) They have quite different tastes for ice cream.

P57 WORKING WITH SCATTER DIAGRAMS

1) a) b)

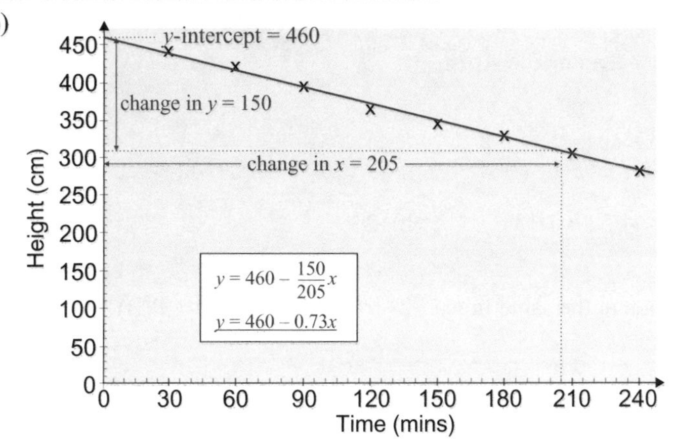

Answers

P58 INTERPOLATION AND EXTRAPOLATION

Plot the points on a graph and draw in the line of best fit.

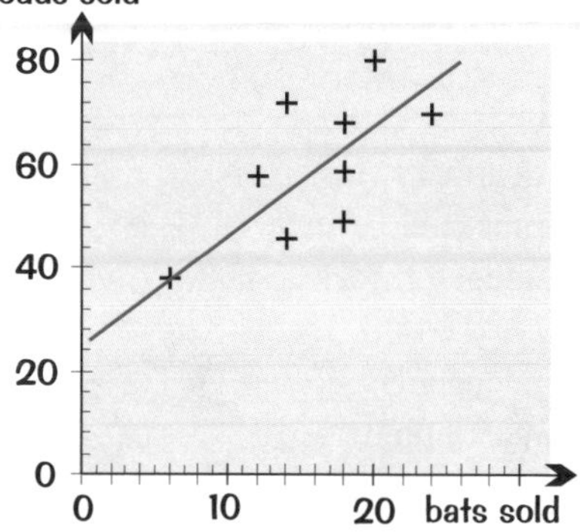

1) All answers need to be sensible figures (i.e. whole numbers) and be consistent with your line of best fit.
   a) accept 9 -11 bats
   b) Equation of my line of best fit is $y = 2.2x + 24$
      So, number of toads = $y = (2.2 \times 32) + 24 = 94.4$, they expect to sell 94 toads (accept 80-100).
   c) $180 = 2.2x + 24$, $x = 70.9$, they expect to sell 71 bats (accept 65-85).

P59 ESTIMATION OF POPULATION

1) a) 15% b) 150 000 c) 35 000

SECTION FOUR — PROBABILITY

P61 PROBABILITY

1) HHH, HHT, HTH, HTT, THH, THT, TTH, TTT
2) a) fairly certain – about 0.95 b) depends on the individual – in a group about half will – 0.5
   c) again depends on the individual answering – let's hope so!

P62 PROBABILITY

1) The probability of a pink poodle winning is 5/8 or 0.625.

P63 SAMPLE SPACE AND VENN DIAGRAMS

1)

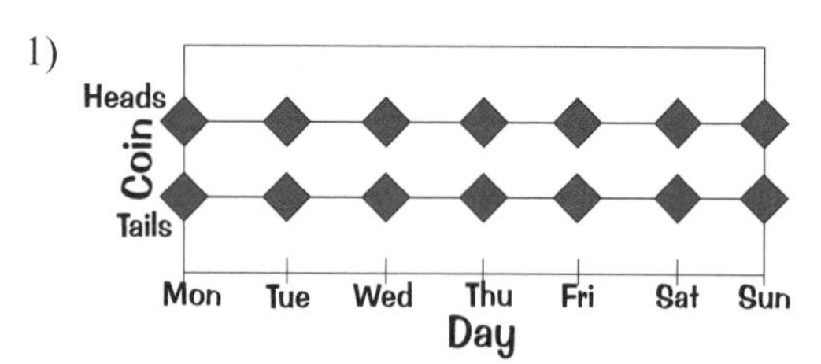

2) Probability of having had soup is 9/32.

P64 EXPECTED FREQUENCIES

1) $1/6 \times 24 = 4$ 2) a) $4/52 = 1/13$ b) 2

P65 PROBABILITY LAWS

1) Events are mutually exclusive if they can't happen at the same time. 2) P(A or B) = P(A) + P(B) – P(A and B)

P66 PROBABILITY LAWS

1) P(A and B) = P(A) × P(B), P(A and B) = P(A) × P(B given that A occurs) 2) $1/6 \times 1/2 = 1/12$
3) $4/52 \times 3/51 = 1/221$

P67 TREE DIAGRAMS AND CONDITIONAL PROBABILITY

1) $1 - 3/20 = 17/20$ 2) $1 - (2/3)^5 = 211/243$

P68 DISCRETE PROBABILITY DISTRIBUTIONS

1) $10(1/4)^3(3/4)^2 = 45/512$

Index

Index

MSHR41